Cassandra Data Modeling & Schema Design and Vector Search

Steve Hoberman

Betul O'Reilly

Align > Refine > Design Series

Technics Publications

Published by:

115 Linda Vista, Sedona, AZ 86336 USA
https://www.TechnicsPub.com

Edited by Sadie Hoberman
Cover design by Lorena Molinari
Illustrations by Joseph Shepherd
Contributions by Pascal Desmarets

First Printing 2024
Copyright © 2024 by Technics Publications

ISBN, print ed.	9781634623155
ISBN, Kindle ed.	9781634623209
ISBN, ePub ed.	9781634623216
ISBN, PDF ed.	9781634623223

Library of Congress Control Number: 2024930200

Contents

List of Figures

List of Tables

About the Book

My daughter can make a mean brownie. She starts with a store-bought brownie mix and adds chocolate chips, apple cider vinegar, and other "secret" ingredients to make her own unique delicious brownie.

Building a robust database design meeting users' needs requires a similar approach. The store-bought brownie mix represents a proven recipe for success. Likewise, there are data modeling practices that have proven successful over many decades. The chocolate chips and other secret ingredients represent the special additions that lead to an exceptional product. Cassandra has a number of special design considerations, much like the chocolate chips. Combining proven data modeling practices with Cassandra design-specific practices creates a series of data models representing powerful communication tools, greatly improving the opportunities for an exceptional design and application.

In fact, each book in the Align > Refine > Design series covers conceptual, logical, and physical data modeling for a specific database product, combining the best of data modeling practices with solution-specific design considerations. It is a winning combination.

My daughter's first few brownies were not a success, although as the proud (and hungry) dad, I ate them anyway—and they were still pretty tasty. It took practice to get the brownie to come out amazing. We need practice on the modeling side as well. Therefore, each book in the series follows the same animal shelter case study, allowing you to see the modeling techniques applied to reinforce your learning.

If you want to learn how to build multiple database solutions, read all the books in the series. Once you read one, you can pick up the techniques for another database solution even quicker.

Some say my first word was "data". I have been a data modeler for over 30 years and have taught variations of my **Data Modeling Master Class** since 1992—currently up to the 10th Edition! I have written nine books on data modeling, including *The Rosedata Stone* and *Data Modeling Made Simple*. I review data models using my Data Model Scorecard® technique. I am the founder of the Design Challenges group, creator of the Data Modeling Institute's Data Modeling Certification exam, Conference Chair of the Data Modeling Zone conferences, director of Technics Publications, lecturer at Columbia University, and recipient of the Data Administration Management Association (DAMA) International Professional Achievement Award.

Thinking of my daughter's brownie analogy, I have perfected the store-bought brownie recipe. That is, I know how to model. However, I am not an expert in every database solution. That is why each book in this series combines my proven data modeling practices with database solution experts. So, for this book, Betul and I are making the brownie together. I work on the store-bought brownie piece, and Betul works on adding the chocolate chips and other delicious ingredients.

Betul O'Reilly is a Solutions Architect at DataStax. She is an experienced Solutions Architect with a strong focus on

Cassandra and relational data modeling. Before her role at DataStax, Betul was Principal Cloud Solution Architect at Oracle, planning, designing, and implementing data and artificial intelligence (AI) solutions for EMEA clients. With 20 years of experience in the telecom, finance, e-commerce, and IT sectors, Betul has established herself as a dynamic figure in data management, analytics, and data science.

We hope our tag team approach shows you how to model any Cassandra solution. Particularly for those with experience in data modeling of relational databases, the book provides a bridge from the traditional methods to the very different way we model to leverage the benefits of NoSQL in general and Cassandra in particular.

About DataStax

In the domain of enterprise-grade solutions based on Apache Cassandra, a robust NoSQL distributed database management system, DataStax stands out as a leading technology provider. With a focus on applications that demand fault tolerance, large-scale distributed data management, and high availability, DataStax has played a key role since its founding in 2010 in helping enterprises use Cassandra's scalability and solid performance. DataStax is known for:

- **DataStax Enterprise (DSE):** Designed specifically for enterprise-level deployments, DSE is a commercial version of Apache Cassandra that includes features like advanced security, advanced indexing and search, and advanced analytics.

- **Astra DB:** Eliminates the challenges related to managing infrastructure during Cassandra deployment thanks to its status as a fully managed, cloud-native database service. It offers scalability and flexibility for cloud applications.

- **Developer Tools:** DataStax offers a range of tools and integrations, such as Kubernetes operator for automated deployment and management, and drivers for other programming languages to make it much easier to develop using Cassandra.

- **DataStax Luna:** Provides knowledge and help to businesses who use the open-source database system Cassandra through a subscription-based support service.

Financial services, retail, healthcare, and the Internet of Things (IoT) are just a few industries that rely on DataStax's solutions for resilient, scalable, and efficient data management. Their commitment to making Cassandra more accessible and manageable for enterprises has made them a leading player in the NoSQL database space.

About Cassandra

Let's cover how different industries use Cassandra's architecture and features. Learn how you can use it to access data. After reading this section, you will also understand how distributed databases work and when to use them. Apache Cassandra stands out as a strong and scalable NoSQL database, capable of managing large amounts of data distributed over multiple nodes while maintaining continuous access without a single point of failure. In Cassandra, a node signifies an individual instance that holds data.

Cassandra's design originated on Facebook with inspiration from Amazon's DynamoDB and Google's Bigtable. Both systems were pioneers in providing scalable and reliable storage solutions, but they were not without flaws. Cassandra combines the strengths of both systems, supporting massive data volumes and efficiently handling intensive queries. Cassandra was released as an open-source project in 2008. It became a top Apache Foundation project in 2010 after joining the Apache Incubator in 2009. Cassandra evolved to be the database solution of choice for many companies, like Apple, Instagram, Uber, Spotify, Facebook, and Netflix.

Traditional relational databases struggle with limited scalability as data grows, lack flexibility due to rigid schemas, and may prioritize strict consistency over availability and scalability. Moreover, large-scale deployments might be expensive to license and maintain. Cassandra, on the other hand, maintains large amounts of data efficiently across multiple nodes, ensuring high availability and eliminating single points of failure. This flexibility includes handling structured, semi-structured, and unstructured data, making it ideal for high-performance use cases. Cassandra shines in write-intensive applications, allowing for fast writes without sacrificing performance or availability. Another great thing about Cassandra is its elastic scalability. When data volume and traffic increase, Cassandra clusters can easily scale up or down to accommodate the change.[1]

Cassandra use cases

Cassandra is a powerful and flexible database system, but it may not be the ideal solution for every application. Use Cassandra if your application requires:

- Handling massive amounts of data across many nodes, providing high availability and no single point of failure. If your application can work on a

---

[1] https://cassandra.apache.org/doc/latest/cassandra/architecture/overview.html.

database with just one server, you might reconsider using Cassandra.

- Excellent in write-intensive workloads due to its distributed architecture. However, a relational database is the way to go if your application handles heavy analytical workloads or has complex queries.

- High availability with no single point of failure, meaning that even if one node fails, the system will continue to function without interruption.

- Replicating data quickly everywhere, regardless of location. You can achieve a high standard of fault tolerance by replicating data across many datacenters, guaranteeing that data is secure even during outages. This strategic distribution of data also leads to low latency.

Cassandra is very flexible, so you can apply it to many use cases:[2]

- **E-commerce and inventory management:** E-commerce companies need a website that is always up and running, especially during peak periods, to

---

[2] https://www.geeksforgeeks.org/system-design-when-to-and-when-not-to-use-cassandra/ and https://www.datastax.com/blog/exploring-common-apache-cassandra-use-cases.

avoid financial losses. They also need a database that can handle a large amount of data and adjust quickly to meet customer expectations. To achieve this, they need to be able to scale their online inventory quickly and cost-effectively. To provide a seamless user experience, e-commerce websites must be fast and scalable.

- **Personalization, recommendations, and customer experience:** Today, we see personalization and recommendation systems everywhere. It's like having built-in helpers in apps and websites that tell us about events or articles we might enjoy. The Eventbrite phone app now uses Cassandra instead of MySQL to tell people about nearby fun events. Vector search can also significantly help e-commerce by improving product recommendations and search functionality. Vector search can help by making searching products and product recommendations easier. It can look at embeddings and keywords to analyze the similarity of items and user preferences. Vector search can show customers more relevant products based on how they've behaved and what they like, improving the user experience and ultimately leading to more sales. Vector search can also quickly and easily handle large catalogs of products and complex queries.

- **Internet of Things (IoT) and edge computing:**
  Keeping an eye on the weather, traffic, energy use,
  stock levels, health signs, video game scores,
  farming conditions, and many other things uses
  sensors, wearable tech, cars, machines, drones, and
  more to make a constant stream of data. We must
  gather this information from reliable devices and
  monitor continuously. Cassandra is a great choice
  for the Internet of Things because it can handle a lot
  of data from many devices at once. It spreads this
  data across many nodes so it doesn't get
  overwhelmed. Additionally, it stores and retrieves
  data very quickly, which is significant for the
  Internet of Things (IoT), where speed is essential.

- **Fraud detection and authentication:** Companies
  need a lot of data to prevent unauthorized user
  access. They must constantly analyze big and varied
  data sets to find unusual patterns that might mean
  fraud. This is especially important in finance,
  banking, payments, and insurance. Another
  important part is confirming people's identities.
  Authentication is critical to every application. The
  challenge is to make this process quick and easy
  while still being sure about who they are. Like fraud
  detection, this needs real-time analysis of lots of
  different data. And since authentication is a big part
  of your systems, you can't afford any breakdowns.

Cassandra architecture

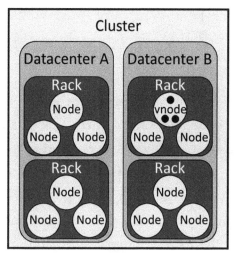

Figure 1: The Cassandra architecture.

Node and Vnode

A node is an individual instance that holds data. Think of it as a basic building block of a Cassandra cluster. Every node, whether a physical or virtual machine, can process both read and write requests, regardless of the data's location within the cluster. Each node functions autonomously but plays an equal role in the overarching system, with Cassandra organizing them in a collaborative *peer-to-peer* manner.

There are also virtual nodes (vnodes). Cassandra uses vnodes to improve data distribution across nodes with more precision. Every vnode stands for a specific data segment within the cluster. By default, each node in

Cassandra has 256 virtual nodes. The use of vnodes allows for flexible data distribution and easier cluster expansion.

Rack

A rack represents a subset of nodes within a datacenter, usually corresponding to a physical rack in a data center. The rack is used to optimize data replication and reduce the risk of data loss. For example, Cassandra tries to place replicas of data on different racks within the same data center. By understanding the rack configuration, Cassandra can intelligently distribute replicas to minimize the impact of a rack-level failure (like the failure of a network switch or power source affecting all nodes on the rack).

Datacenter

A datacenter in Cassandra typically refers to a collection of nodes located in a single physical location or providing a specific type of service (like analytics or search). Cassandra supports multiple datacenters, and each datacenter can have multiple nodes. When there is more than one logical datacenter configured in a cluster, Cassandra will place copies of the data (replicas) on distinct datacenters. This helps to ensure that if one datacenter goes down, the data is still available on other datacenters. Datacenters provide additional levels of fault tolerance and ensure that data is distributed evenly across the cluster. Using datacenters is an important part of Cassandra's architecture and helps ensure that data is always available and that the cluster is fault-tolerant.

Cluster

A cluster refers to a network of interconnected nodes that collectively manage and store data. It can span multiple datacenters, each representing a collection of nodes typically located in the same physical or cloud region. Unlike traditional hierarchical systems, all nodes in a Cassandra cluster function equally, avoiding master-slave dynamics. The cluster distributes data uniformly across nodes using a specific partitioning strategy, and it replicates data to guarantee high availability and resilience against failures. The structure is easily scalable; adding new nodes to the cluster doesn't disrupt existing operations. Cassandra clusters can also be tailored for awareness of datacenters and racks, enhancing the efficiency of data replication and accessibility over diverse geographic areas. This non-centralized approach ensures the cluster is not vulnerable to single points of failure, offering robust reliability for managing data on a large scale.

Data replication

In Cassandra, data replication involves creating multiple copies of data and distributing the data across different nodes in a cluster, ensuring high availability and fault tolerance. When data is written to a node, it is automatically replicated to other nodes based on a predefined replication factor, which dictates the number of replicas. This replication strategy ensures that even in the event of node failures, data remains accessible and secure, contributing to Cassandra's robustness with large-scale distributed data.

DC1 RF=3

Node	Primary	Replica	Replica
Node 1	00-25	76-100	51-75
Node 2	26-50	00-25	76-100
Node 3	51-75	25-50	00-25
Node 4	76-100	51-75	26-50

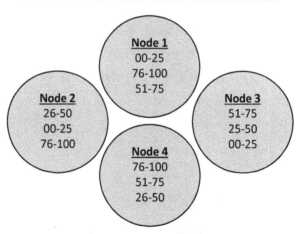

Figure 2: Data replication.

We can determine the number of replicas and their location by the replication factor and replication strategy. The replication factor is the total number of replicas across the cluster. When we set this factor to one, only one copy of each row exists in a cluster. We can set this replication factor for each keyspace at the datacenter level. A keyspace in Cassandra is the top-level data container, similar to a schema in relational database systems. It is the primary namespace used to organize and access your data.

```
CREATE KEYSPACE my_keyspace WITH replication =
{'class': 'NetworkTopologyStrategy',
'datacenter1': 3, 'datacenter2': 3};
```

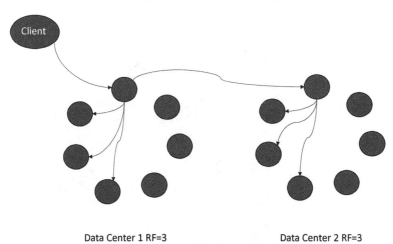

Data Center 1 RF=3   Data Center 2 RF=3

Figure 3: Replication factor.

The replication strategy controls how the replicas are chosen. Cassandra has two strategies for determining which nodes contain replicated data. The *SimpleStrategy* is unaware of the logical division of nodes for datacenters and racks. The *NetworkTopologyStrategy*, is more complicated and is both racks-aware and datacenter-aware. Use the *NetworkTopologyStrategy* if your cluster is set up in multiple datacenters or if you intend to do so in the future. This approach lets you define the number of copies of your data in each datacenter. We can define how many replicas to place in different data centers by using the *NetworkTopologyStrategy*.

Data distribution

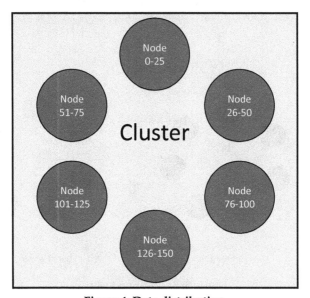

Figure 4: Data distribution.

At its core, Cassandra's architecture is designed around the principles of partitioning. Data within Cassandra is partitioned across multiple nodes in a cluster. Each partition holds a subset of the data, determined by the partition key defined for the data model. We use this key to hash and distribute data evenly across the nodes, allowing for horizontal scaling and efficient utilization of resources.

pet_id	pet_name	species	breed	age
98e5ca92-20d0-47b9-8a1c-3eaad566f23b	Max	Dog	Golden Retriever	3
98e5ca92-20d0-47b9-8a1c-3eaad566f23b	Luna	Cat	Siamese	2
72e83378-6e3c-4f6a-9c63-582f1805f5e4	Bella	Dog	Poodle	2
f7d9eb55-27c8-4d13-bae0-1e03a2767b20	Whiskers	Cat	Maine Coon	4

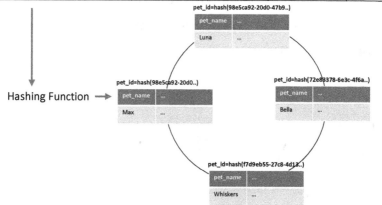

Figure 5: Cassandra's distributed architecture[3]

By distributing data across nodes, Cassandra achieves both load balancing and fault tolerance, as it stores data replicas on different nodes in the cluster. Each partition is replicated across multiple nodes to ensure data availability and resilience against node failures. This distribution and

[3] https://www.datastax.com/resources/whitepaper/data-modeling-apache-cassandra.

replication method improves performance and ensures that data is available even if hardware or network problems happen. In this way, Cassandra's distributed architecture and partitioning mechanism provide manage large datasets in a scalable and fault-tolerant manner.

CAP Theorem

Understanding the CAP (Consistency, Availability, Partition Tolerance) theorem is important when considering Cassandra's architecture and data modeling.

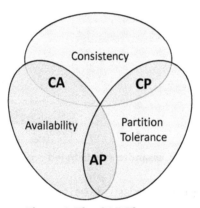

Figure 6: The CAP Theorem.

According to the CAP theorem, by Eric Brewer, you can only guarantee two of these three characteristics when storing data across many systems:[4]

---

[4] https://en.wikipedia.org/wiki/CAP_theorem.

- **Consistency:** The data must be consistent even after executing an operation. This means every read request in the future should include the written data. When you change the status of an order, for example, everyone should see the new state.

- **Availability:** Database availability and responsiveness should be always guaranteed. There should be zero downtime.

- **Partition tolerance:** The system continues to function normally if a part of the messages is dropped or there is delayed network latency between nodes.

Cassandra prioritizes partition tolerance and availability over strict consistency. The CAP theorem defines an AP (Availability and Partition Tolerant) system as one that compromises strong consistency to achieve high availability and fault tolerance. This is addressed by enabling eventual consistency, which implies that all updates will eventually reach all replicas. Users can adjust the levels of consistency. Users can balance consistency, performance, and availability in this way.

Tunable consistency

You can modify the consistency of the data using Cassandra. You can choose the level of consistency while reading or saving data. That is, you determine the number of copies of the data required to validate the operation before the completion of the operation. For example, you generally don't need the most recent data if you're counting the number of "likes" on a post. Cassandra will, therefore, get a value from the nearest replica if you specify a low consistency level, such as ONE. However, you can select a higher level, such as TWO, THREE, or QUORUM, if you want to be certain of the facts. A majority of the copies must agree to have quorum. You will view the most recent data if all are consistent, and the data contains a high degree of consistency. When data is read from replicas and there are differences, Cassandra will internally handle a procedure to ensure that replicas are up-to-date and synchronized.

This also applies when saving data. A high consistency level requires many copies of the data to be saved before finishing. For instance, if you select "ALL" or "THREE" for a table with three copies, each copy must save the data before completion. However, if you choose a high consistency level and a copy is down or unavailable, the action will fail because Cassandra cannot meet the specified level, sacrificing availability to ensure consistency.[5]

---

[5] https://www.datastax.com/blog/how-apache-cassandratm-balances-consistency-availability-and-performance.

ACID transactions at scale

In Cassandra Version 5, ACID transactions will be possible through a new consensus protocol called Accord. A white paper authored by three researchers from Apple (Benedict Elliot Smith, Blake Eggleston, and Scott Andreas), and Tony Zhang from the University of Michigan, covers this feature.[6]

Cassandra features

We've already covered the cluster and node aspects of the Cassandra architecture. Now, let's dive into keyspace, column family/tables, rows, and columns.

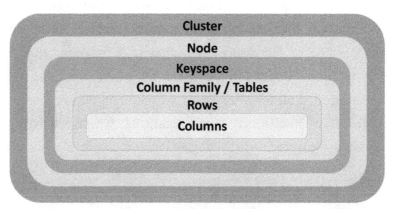

Figure 7: Cassandra features.

---

[6] https://cwiki.apache.org/confluence/download/attachments/188744725/Accord.pdf?version=2&modificationDate=1637000779000&api=v2.

Keyspace

A keyspace in Cassandra is a top-level container that organizes and manages related data within the cluster. It's a way to combine tables and data for specific applications or purposes. Think of it as a sort of "namespace" for data, similar to a schema in relational databases. Each keyspace defines the configuration settings, replication strategy, and other attributes that determine how the data stored within it is managed and distributed across the nodes in the Cassandra cluster. In other words, a keyspace sets the rules for storing, replicating, and retrieving data. This separation allows you to isolate and control different data or application domains within the same Cassandra cluster, providing flexibility, scalability, and ease of management in dealing with datasets. It is common to create one keyspace per application. It ensures logical data separation, allows for tailored replication and configuration settings per application, simplifies schema management, and enhances security with distinct access controls within its own dedicated keyspace.

```
CREATE KEYSPACE my_keyspace WITH replication =
{'class': 'NetworkTopologyStrategy',
'datacenter1': 3, 'datacenter2': 2};
```

Table/Column Family

In Cassandra's CQL (Cassandra Query Language version), a table is like a table in a traditional relational database. It's a structured data container that exists inside a keyspace. We define columns in a CQL table with specific data types such as text, integer, or timestamp. Each table contains rows and columns, where a unique primary key identifies each row. The primary key consists of one or more columns. More on keys:

- **Partition Key**: The part of the primary key that determines what node the partition is stored on. Without a partition key in the where clause, the data scan will result in an inefficient full cluster scan by using ALLOW FILTERING. If there is only one column in the primary key, it is called a Single Primary key, which only consists of the partition key. Creating a Composite Partition key, which involves multiple columns, is also possible. It is an effective strategy for a table to prevent hotspotting. This approach divides the data into smaller, more manageable chunks.

- **Clustering Key**: It sorts the data within the partition.

- **Primary Key**: It includes the partition key and any/all clustering columns. In Cassandra, an upsert is a natural operation because of its distributed, NoSQL nature. Cassandra does not differentiate between an insert and an update at the data manipulation level. They are both essentially write operations. If the record already exists with the same primary key, you will lose the older data version, so it is important to choose the primary key carefully.

```
CREATE TABLE (
    COLUMN TYPE [STATIC],                    STATIC is optional
    COLUMN TYPE [STATIC],
    ...,
    ...,
    ...,                                     Partition Key and Optional
    PRIMARY KEY ((COLUMN,COLUMN),[COLUMN,..])    Clustering Key
) WITH CLUSTERING ORDER BY (
        CLUSTERING_COLUMN [ASC|DESC],...     Row ordering in a partition
);
```

Figure 8: About tables.

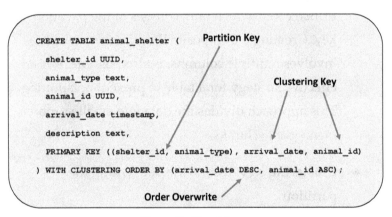

```
CREATE TABLE animal_shelter (          Partition Key

    shelter_id UUID,

    animal_type text,                                Clustering Key

    animal_id UUID,

    arrival_date timestamp,

    description text,

    PRIMARY KEY ((shelter_id, animal_type), arrival_date, animal_id)
) WITH CLUSTERING ORDER BY (arrival_date DESC, animal_id ASC);
```

Order Overwrite

Figure 9: About keys.

The above primary key consists of two parts:

- The composite partition key (**shelter_id** and **animal_type**) helps the distribution across the cluster based on **shelter** and **animal type**.

- The clustering columns (**arrival_date** and **animal_id**) will define the order of data within each partition. **Arrival_date** is ordered in descending order (newest first), and **animal_id** is ordered in ascending order.

Columns

The fundamental building block of data storage in a table is a column. A schema is fixed in the relational model. Once you define the columns for a table, every row in that table must have values for all the defined columns, even if some of them are null in relational databases. However, Cassandra takes a different approach. While tables are defined, there is no requirement for all rows to have the same set of columns, providing greater flexibility in data modeling.

In a row, each column is named and paired with a value that uniquely identifies it. Components of the column are:

- Column name
- Column value
- Timestamp
- TTL(Optional)

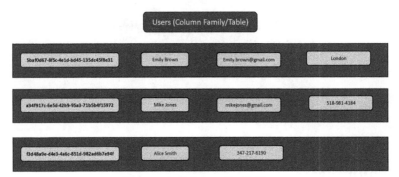

Figure 10: Column flexibility.

Timestamp

When you insert or update data in a Cassandra table, each write operation includes a timestamp based on the system's internal clock. The timestamp value returned by WRITETIME() represents when the column was last written or updated. It's important to note that the system manages these timestamps, and they exist for internal purposes like conflict resolution and time-based ordering.

```
shelter_id            |  animal_id               |  writetime(description)
------------------    |  ----------------------  |  ---------------------
c0789be1-a23d-4bbc-   |  516f9651-98d4-4e71-bd89- |  1691933480270477
8c6e-760a772364d7        e17a227e3f48

3596bee9-fbd8-42c3-   |  7ed4ba72-8280-41d9-ba6f- |  1691933480287389
8ab7-4d44280ed0e9        51fac8603f5d

98e86292-31a0-4538-   |  c563edc6-2906-4e42-a9e6- |  1691933480292435
aa03-1110521b5fbe        c989339beacb

fc10a500-5bba-435e-   |  e2bd6d7c-b681-4c91-8258- |  1691933531405005
84ed-3226106d6245        3ca4dd8e881b
```

Figure 11: Writetime of description column.

The *writetime* can be different for each column within the same row. The *writetime* is a timestamp that indicates when a particular piece of data was written. When you update or insert data into specific columns, Cassandra stores a separate *writetime* for each of those columns. This allows you to track when each individual piece of data was last updated, which can be useful for data auditing, conflict resolution, or time-based data analysis.

Time to Live (TTL)

In Cassandra, Time to Live (TTL) is a feature that allows you to specify how long we need to retain data in the database. When you set a TTL for a specific piece of data, Cassandra will ensure that the data is automatically removed from the database after the specified time has elapsed. TTL can be useful in scenarios where you have data that becomes irrelevant or outdated after a certain period of time. Instead of manually deleting this data, you can set a TTL to automatically let Cassandra handle its expiration. When you insert data with a TTL, the TTL value is associated with that piece of data. Cassandra will keep track of the timestamp when the data was inserted and the TTL value. When the TTL expires, Cassandra's built-in compaction process will remove the data during the regular maintenance cycle. If you define TTL for a table, if any column exceeds TTL, the entire table is tombstoned.

```
CREATE TABLE animal_shelter
```

```
(shelter_id UUID,
  animal_type TEXT,
  animal_id UUID,
  arrival_date TIMESTAMP,
  description TEXT,
  PRIMARY KEY (shelter_id, animal_id)
) WITH default_time_to_live = 3600;

-- Insert with TTL of 1 day (86400 seconds)
INSERT INTO animal_shelter (shelter_id,
animal_type, animal_id, arrival_date, description)
VALUES (uuid(), 'Dog', uuid(), '2023-08-10
12:00:00', 'Friendly Labrador') USING TTL 86400;
```

You can also define TTL for a row. In this example, the data you're inserting will be automatically deleted from the animal_shelter table after one day (86400 seconds) from the insertion time. You can check how much longer the data will live with TTL function:

```
SELECT TTL(shelter_id) FROM animal_shelter WHERE
shelter_id = 104;
```

Denormalization

Joins cannot be implemented in Cassandra's distributed setup because they contradict the database's core objectives of scalability and high performance across multiple nodes. Cassandra distributes its data across multiple nodes in a cluster. To perform a join, these nodes would need to coordinate closely to gather and process the data, which would significantly add to the network overhead and cause delays. The distributed architecture of Cassandra, which allows each node to operate independently and effectively, would be compromised by this complex procedure. As a result, Cassandra avoids joins in favor of data modeling techniques like denormalization, which support the performance and scalability of its distributed

Since Cassandra has no joins, you can prepare all the data you need in one denormalized table. It is normal to have one table per query in Cassandra. Denormalization is important for achieving high read and write performance. Unlike traditional relational databases, which try to reduce data redundancy through normalization, Cassandra encourages data duplication to optimize query performance.

When you denormalize data, you're optimizing for read operations by storing redundant data to make it readily accessible from multiple points in the cluster. This can eliminate the need for complex joins and multiple queries, which are not natively supported or can be performance-intensive in distributed systems like Cassandra. Additionally, denormalization allows you to create tables tailored for specific query patterns, further enhancing data retrieval speed. By strategically denormalizing your data, you can ensure that read and write operations are as fast and efficient as possible.

CQL

CQL (Cassandra Query Language) is the query language of Apache Cassandra. Even though CQL is similar to SQL and easy to adapt, there are many differences.

With Hackolade Studio, it is easy in the data model to generate the CQL script to create keyspaces, tables with columns with their data types and other properties, and indexes. It is also easy to reverse-engineer a CQL script or database instance to generate an entity-relationship diagram for documentation purposes, or to make the model evolve continuously according to application changes.

The primary key defines data uniqueness. The partition key organizes how to distribute data. The partition key is the most important to decide while designing data modeling in Cassandra. The size of a partition ideally could be around 10MB and a max of 100MB. The size is important because it will affect your write and read performance. To ensure optimal performance in Cassandra, it is advisable to evenly distribute data across cluster nodes. This involves defining data partitions in a way that promotes their balanced distribution across the entire cluster, rather than concentrating them on just a few nodes.

Partitions are collections of rows that share a common partition key. When retrieving data from Cassandra, the goal is to minimize the number of partitions read. Reading from multiple partitions is consistently more resource-intensive than reading from a single partition. On the other hand, you must create an index if you want to filter on a column that is not a primary or partition key. Clustering keys can also allow inequality predicates and ordering.

Here is how to design the table to access with a shelter_id filter. We would need to change the partition key to animal_type:

```
CREATE TABLE animalshelter_by_shelter_id (
   shelter_id UUID,
   animal_type text,
   animal_id UUID,
   arrival_date timestamp,
   description text,
   PRIMARY KEY (shelter_id, animal_type,
arrival_date)
) WITH CLUSTERING ORDER BY (animal_type DESC,
arrival_date ASC);
```

```
SELECT * FROM animalshelter_by_shelter_id WHERE
shelter_id = c1b52dd9-771a-4f8b-b173-13a903c4295f
;
```

Here is how to design the table to access with an animal_type filter:

```
CREATE TABLE animalshelter_by_animal_type(
   shelter_id UUID,
   animal_type text,
   animal_id UUID,
   arrival_date timestamp,
   description text,
   PRIMARY KEY ( animal_type, shelter_id,
arrival_date)
) WITH CLUSTERING ORDER BY (shelter_id DESC,
arrival_date ASC);
```

```
SELECT * FROM animalshelter_by_animal_type  WHERE
animal_type='Dog';
```

Let's look at queries for the *animal_shelter_by_animal_type* table. These are correct CQL statements, as the partition is in the filter with an equality predicate:

```
SELECT * FROM animalshelter_by_animal_type WHERE
shelter_id = c1b52dd9-771a-4f8b-b173-13a903c4295f
AND animal_type = 'Dog'
AND arrival_date >= '2023-08-01' AND arrival_date
<= '2023-08-15';

SELECT * FROM animalshelter_by_animal_type WHERE
shelter_id = c1b52dd9-771a-4f8b-b173-13a903c4295f
AND animal_type = 'Dog';
```

These are incorrect CQL statements, as the partition is not in the filter predicate or involves data filtering. It can only work with ALLOW FILTERING:

```
SELECT * FROM animalshelter_by_animal_type WHERE
shelter_id = c1b52dd9-771a-4f8b-b173-13a903c4295f;

SELECT * FROM animalshelter_by_animal_type WHERE
shelter_id = c1b52dd9-771a-4f8b-b173-13a903c4295f
AND animal_type = 'Dog' and description='German
Shepherds';
```

Data deletion and tombstones

Data deletion in Cassandra is different from relational databases due to the distributed nature of Cassandra. A delete operation is treated as an insert or upsert operation and adds a deletion marker called a tombstone. Tombstones mark deleted data and are managed through a compaction process after a certain time (gc_grace_period). Tombstones take up disk space and can cause performance issues if not managed properly. Tombstones are not only created by deletes. They can be also created by:

- DELETE statements.
- Setting Time to Live(TTLs)
- Inserting null values
- Inserting data into parts of a collection.

After creating a tombstone, we can mark on different parts of a partition. Based on the location of the marker, we can categorize tombstones into one of the following groups:[7]

- **Partition tombstones:** We generate partition tombstones when we delete an entire partition explicitly. In the CQL DELETE statement, the WHERE clause is an equality condition against the partition key.

- **Row tombstones:** We generate row tombstones when explicitly deleting a particular row within a partition. The schema has a composite primary key that includes both partition and clustering keys. In the CQL DELETE statement, the WHERE clause is an equality condition against both partition and clustering key columns.

---

[7] https://docs.datastax.com/en/dse/5.1/docs/architecture/database-internals/architecture-tombstones.html.

- **Range tombstones:** Range tombstones occur when several rows within a partition that we can express through a range search are deleted explicitly. The schema has a composite primary key that includes both partition and clustering keys. In the CQL DELETE statement, the WHERE clause is an equality condition against the partition key, plus an inequality condition against the clustering key.

- **Complex column tombstones:** We generate these when inserting or updating a collection type column, such as set, list, or map.

- **Cell tombstones:** We generate cell tombstones when explicitly deleting a value from a cell, such as a column for a specific partition row or when inserting or updating a cell with null values.

- **TTL tombstones:** We generate TTL tombstones when the TTL (time-to-live) period expires. The TTL expiration marker can occur at either the row or cell level.

Alter Operations in CQL

You can change the datatype of a column in a table, add new columns, drop existing columns, rename columns, and change table properties:

```
ALTER TABLE [keyspace_name.] table_name
```

```
[ALTER column_name TYPE cql_type]
[ADD (column_definition_list)]
[DROP column_list | COMPACT STORAGE ]
[RENAME column_name TO column_name]
[WITH table_properties];
```

You can modify the keyspace replication strategy, the number of copies of the data Cassandra creates in each datacenter, REPLICATION, or disable the commit log for writes, DURABLE_WRITES:

```
ALTER KEYSPACE keyspace_name
   WITH REPLICATION = {
      'class' : 'SimpleStrategy',
'replication_factor' : N
      | 'class' : 'NetworkTopologyStrategy',
'dc1_name' : N [,...]
      }
   [AND DURABLE_WRITES =  true|false] ;
```

You can modify an existing user-defined type (UDT):

```
ALTER TYPE field_name
[ALTER field_name TYPE new_cql_datatype
| ADD (field_name cql_datatype[,...])
| RENAME field_name TO new_field_name[AND ...]]⁸
```

With Hackolade Studio, when comparing two data models (or two versions of the same model), it is easy to generate the ALTER script from a delta model. Modifying users, roles, and materialized views in Cassandra is also possible.

---

⁸ https://docs.datastax.com/en/cql-
oss/3.3/cql/cql_reference/cqlAlterType.html.

Cassandra data types

Table 1 contains the built-in data types for columns.

Data Type	Description
Ascii	Stores string: US-ASCII character string
Bigint	Stores integers: 64-bit signed long
Blob	Stores blob: Arbitrary bytes, expressed as hexadecimal
Counter	Stores integers: Distributed counter value (64-bit long)
Date	Store strings: Value is a date with no corresponding time value; Cassandra encodes date as a 32-bit integer representing days since epoch (January 1, 1970). We can represent dates in queries and inserts as a string, such as 2015-05-03 (yyyy-mm-dd)
Decimal	Stores integers, floats: Variable-precision decimal.
Double	Stores integers, floats: 64-bit IEEE-754 floating point
Float	Stores integers, floats: 32-bit IEEE-754 floating point
frozen	Used for user-defined types, collections, tuples: A frozen value serializes multiple components into a single value. Non-frozen types allow updates to individual fields. Cassandra treats the value of a frozen type as a blob. The entire value must be overwritten.
Inet	Stores strings: IP address string in IPv4 or IPv6 format, used by the python-cql driver and CQL native protocols
int	Stores integers: 32-bit signed integer
List	A collection of one or more ordered elements: [literal, literal, literal].
Map	A JSON-style array of literals: { literal : literal, literal : literal ... }
Set	A collection of one or more elements: { literal, literal, literal }
smallint	2-byte integer
text	UTF-8 encoded string
time	Value is encoded as a 64-bit signed integer representing the number of nanoseconds since midnight. Values can be represented as strings, such as 13:30:54.234.
timestamp	Date and time with millisecond precision, encoded as 8 bytes since epoch. Can be represented as a string, such as 2015-05-03 13:30:54.234.

Data Type	Description
timeuuid	Version 1 UUID only
tinyint	1 byte integer
tuple	Cassandra 2.1 and later. A group of 2-3 fields.
uuid	A UUID in standard UUID format
varchar	UTF-8 encoded string
varint	Arbitrary-precision integer
vector	Required for vector search in Cassandra 5 and above. Defined by a fixed-length array of not null 32-bit floating points. Maximum dimension is 8K (2^13) items.

Table 1: Built-in data types[9]

Collection types

Collection types are special kinds of data types that allow you to store multiple values in a single column. There are three main types of collections in CQL:

- **List:** A list is an ordered collection of elements. All the elements must be of the same type. Lists allow duplicates and you can modify them by adding or removing elements.

```
CREATE TABLE my_table (id INT PRIMARY KEY, my_list
LIST<TEXT>);
```

- **Set**: A set is an unordered collection of unique elements. Like lists, all elements must be of the same type. Sets don't allow duplicate values.

---

[9] https://docs.datastax.com/en/cql-oss/3.x/cql/cql_reference/cql_data_types_c.html.

```
CREATE TABLE my_table (id INT PRIMARY KEY, my_set
SET<TEXT>);
```

- **Map:** A map is a collection of key-value pairs. All keys must be of the same type, and all values must also be of the same type, but keys and values can be of different types from each other. Each key in the map is unique.

```
CREATE TABLE my_table (id INT PRIMARY KEY, my_map
MAP<TEXT, INT>);
```

Using the correct collection type is important. Each has its unique features, advantages, and best use cases. Table 2 shows when to use them along with examples.

Collection Type	When to use	Example

LIST	Use a list when you need to keep the order of the elements. Suitable for implementing queues, stacks, or storing ordered records.	It could be storing comments as a list type in the order they were made:
		
		`CREATE TABLE entity_comments (`
		`    entity_id UUID PRIMARY KEY,`
		`    comments list<text>`
		`);`
		
		`INSERT INTO entity_comments`
		`(entity_id, comments) VALUES`
		`(uuid(), ['Great Product', 'Good`
		`for value']);`

SET	When you need a collection of unique elements and the order isn't important, use a set. Suitable for storing non-duplicate data such as tags and categories.	It could be storing tags as a set type to hold unique values:
		
		`CREATE TABLE item_tags (`
		`    item_id UUID PRIMARY KEY,`
		`    tags set<text>`
		`);`
		
		`INSERT INTO item_tags (item_id,`
		`tags) VALUES (uuid(), {'shoes',`
		`'footwear', 'accessories'});`

Collection Type	When to use	Example

MAP	Use a map when you need a simple key-value store within a single row. Suitable for storing JSON-like data structures, metadata, or other associative data.	It could be storing metadata as map type which stores as key-value pairs:
		
		`CREATE TABLE item_metadata (`
		`    item_id UUID PRIMARY KEY,`
		`    metadata map<text, text>`
		`);`
		
		`INSERT INTO item_metadata`
		`(item_id, metadata) VALUES`
		`(uuid(), {'title': ' The`
		`Enchanted Journey', 'author':`
		`'Alice Johnson', 'date': '2023-`
		`03-20'});`

Table 2: Collection types

Another type in Cassandra is a user-defined type (UDT). UDTs let you group multiple related fields into a single column, each with a name and a type. This makes managing complex data structures within a single row in Cassandra easier. For example, let's say you're working on a shopping app and want to store customer addresses. Instead of having separate columns for street, city, state, and zip code, you could create a UDT-named address that contains all these fields.

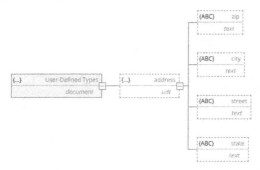

Figure 12: UDT-named address.

```
CREATE TYPE IF NOT EXISTS "Customer".address (
    "zip" text,
    "city" text,
    "street" text,
    "state" text
);
```

Once you create the address type, you can use it in a table like this:

Customers		
customer_id	pk,PK	uuid *
name		text
☐ shipping_address		udt
zip		text
city		text
street		text
state		text
☐ billing_address		udt
zip		text
city		text
street		text
state		text

Figure 13: Table with UDT types

```
CREATE TYPE IF NOT EXISTS address (
    "zip" text,
    "city" text,
    "street" text,
    "state" text
);
CREATE TABLE "Customers" (
    "customer_id" uuid,
    "name" text,
    "shipping_address" frozen<address>,
    "billing_address" frozen<address>,
    PRIMARY KEY ("customer_id")
);
INSERT INTO "Customers" ("customer_id", "name",
"shipping_address", "billing_address") VALUES (
    uuid(),
    'Alice',
```

```
  {"zip": '11111', "city": 'Shipville', "street":
'123 Ship St', "state": 'CA'},
  {"zip": '22222', "city": 'Billville', "street":
'123 Bill St', "state": 'TX'}
);
```

We use the keyword *frozen* when declaring a UDT in a table, indicating that we should treat the UDT as a single, indivisible unit. That means you can't update just one field in a *frozen* UDT; you'd have to overwrite the entire UDT column. UDTs offer a way to keep related data together, making it more organized and easier to manage. For optimal performance, use frozen UDTs and limit the number of fields in non-frozen UDTs. While you can add fields to a UDT, removing them is not an option, making schema changes tricky. We should use UDTs only when necessary, as regular table columns or text blobs are preferable. Try to be cautious while nesting UDTs within other UDTs or collections. Excessive nesting can lead to large mutations, potentially causing table operations to fail if they exceed the maximum mutation size.

Data modeling and schema design

Data modeling, using a tool such as Hackolade Studio, is a crucial step in the development process, as it allows developers to work closely with subject matter experts to define the structure of the data before any coding begins. Just as we use a recipe to guide the baking of brownies, a data model serves as a blueprint for the structure and organization of data. By involving subject matter experts in the modeling process, developers can ensure that the data model accurately reflects the needs and requirements of the project. With such collaboration, developers are more likely to avoid potential mistakes and inconsistencies arising from working with poorly defined data. By following a recipe before starting to bake, developers can be more efficient and successful in creating a product that meets the end-user's needs.

Audience

We wrote this book for two audiences:

- Data architects and modelers who need to expand their modeling skills to include Cassandra. That is, those of us who know how to make a store-bought brownie but are looking for those secret additions like chocolate chips.

- Database administrators and developers who know Cassandra, but need to expand their modeling skills. Those of us who know the value of chocolate chips and other ingredients but need to learn how to combine these ingredients with those store-bought brownie mixes.

This book contains a foundational introduction followed by three approach-driven chapters. Think of the introduction as making that store-built brownie and the subsequent chapters as adding chocolate chips and other yummy ingredients. More on these four sections:

- **Introduction: About Data Models.** This overview covers the three modeling characteristics of precise, minimal, and visual; the three model components of entities, relationships, and attributes; the three model levels of conceptual (align), logical (refine), and physical (design); and the three modeling perspectives of relational, dimensional, and query. By the end of this introduction, you will know data modeling concepts and how to approach any data modeling assignment. This introduction will be useful to database administrators and developers who need a foundation in data modeling, as well as data architects and data modelers who need a modeling refresher.

- **Chapter 1: Align.** This chapter will explain the data modeling align phase. We explain the purpose of aligning our business vocabulary, introduce our animal shelter case study, and then walk through the align approach. This chapter will be useful for both audiences, architects/modelers and database administrators/developers.

- **Chapter 2: Refine**. This chapter will explain the data modeling refine phase. We explain the purpose of refine, refine the model for our animal shelter case study, and then walk through the refine approach. This chapter will be useful for both audiences, architects/modelers and database administrators/developers.

- **Chapter 3: Design**. This chapter will explain the data modeling design phase. We explain the purpose of design, design the model for our animal shelter case study, and then walk through the design approach. This chapter will be useful for both audiences, architects/modelers and database administrators/developers.

We end each chapter with three tips and three takeaways. We aim to write as concisely yet comprehensively as possible to make the most of your time.

Most data models throughout the book were created using Hackolade Studio (https://hackolade.com) and are accessible at https://github.com/hackolade/books, along with additional sample data models to play with.

Let's begin!

Betul and Steve

About Data Models

This chapter is all about making that store-built brownie. We present the data modeling principles and concepts within a single chapter. In addition to explaining the data model, this chapter covers the three modeling characteristics of precise, minimal, and visual; the three model components of entities, relationships, and attributes; the three model levels of conceptual (align), logical (refine), and physical (design); and the three modeling perspectives of relational, dimensional, and query. By the end of this chapter, you will know how to approach any data modeling assignment.

Data model explanation

A model is a precise representation of a landscape. Precise means there is only one way to read a model—it is not ambiguous nor up to interpretation. You and I read the same model the exact same way, making the model an extremely valuable communication tool.

We need to 'speak' a language before we can discuss content. That is, once we know how to read the symbols on a model (syntax), we can discuss what the symbols represent (semantics).

Once we understand the syntax, we can discuss the semantics.

For example, a map like the one in Figure 14 helps a visitor navigate a city. Once we know what the symbols on a map mean, such as lines representing streets, we can read the map and use it as a valuable navigation tool for understanding a geographical landscape.

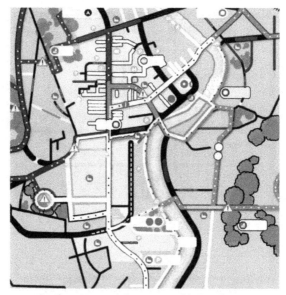

Figure 14: Map of a geographic landscape.

A blueprint like the one in Figure 15 helps an architect communicate building plans. The blueprint, too, contains only representations, such as rectangles for rooms and lines for pipes. Once we know what the rectangles and lines mean on a blueprint, we know what the structure will look like and can understand the architectural landscape.

The data model like the one in Figure 16 helps business professionals and technologists discuss requirements and terminology. The data model, too, contains only representations, such as rectangles for terms and lines for business rules. Once we know what the rectangles and lines mean on a data model, we can debate and eventually agree on the business requirements and terminology captured in the informational landscape.

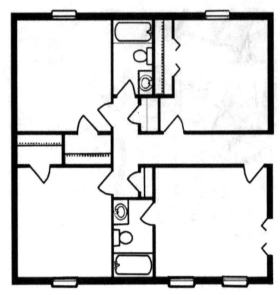

Figure 15: Map of an architectural landscape.

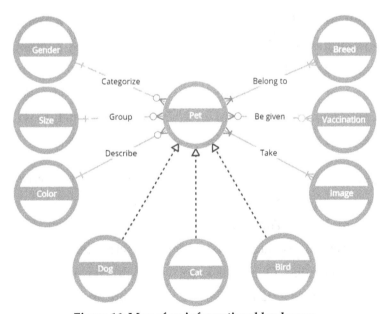

Figure 16: Map of an informational landscape.

A data model is a precise representation of an information landscape. We build data models to confirm and document our understanding of other perspectives.

In addition to precision, two other important characteristics of the model are minimal and visual. Let's discuss all three characteristics.

Three model characteristics

Models are valuable because they are precise—there is only one way to interpret the symbols on the model. We must transform the ambiguity in our verbal and sometimes written communication into a precise language. Precision does not mean complex—we need to keep our language simple and show the minimal amount needed for successful communication. In addition, following the maxim "a picture is worth a thousand words," we need visuals to communicate this precise and simple language for the initiative.

Precise, minimal, and visual are three essential characteristics of the model.

Precise

Bob: How's your course going?

Mary: Going well. But my students are complaining about too much homework. They tell me they have many other classes.

Bob: The attendees in my advanced session say the same thing.

Mary: I wouldn't expect that from graduates. Anyway, how many other offerings are you teaching this semester?

Bob: I'm teaching five offerings this term and one is an evening not-for-credit class.

We can let this conversation continue for a few pages, but do you see the ambiguity caused by this simple dialog?

- What is the difference between **Course**, **Class**, **Offering**, and **Session**?
- Are **Semester** and **Term** the same?
- Are **Student** and **Attendee** the same?

Precision means "exactly or sharply defined or stated." Precision means there is only one interpretation for a term, including the term's name, definition, and connections to other terms. Most issues organizations face related to growth, credibility, and saving lives, stem from a lack of precision.

On a recent project, Steve needed to explain data modeling to a group of senior human resource executives. These very high-level managers lead departments responsible for implementing a very expensive global employee expense system. Steve felt the last thing these busy human resource executives needed was a lecture on data modeling. So, instead, he asked each of these managers sitting around this large boardroom table to write down their definition of an employee. After a few minutes, most of the writing stopped and he asked them to share their definitions of an employee.

As expected, no two definitions were the same. For example, one manager included contingency workers in his definition, while another included summer interns. Instead of spending the remaining meeting time attempting to come to a consensus on the meaning of an employee, we discussed the reasons we create data models, including the value of precision. Steve explained that after we complete the difficult journey of achieving the agreed-upon employee definition and document it in the form of a data model, no one will ever have to go through the same painful process again. Instead, they can use and build upon the existing model, adding even more value for the organization.

Making terms precise is hard work. We need to transform the ambiguity in our verbal and sometimes written communication into a form where five people can read about the term and each gets a single clear picture of the term, not five different interpretations. For example, a group of business users initially define **Product** as:

Something we produce intending to sell for profit.

Is this definition precise? If you and I read this definition, are we each clear on what *something* means? Is *something* tangible like a hammer or instead some type of service? If it is a hammer and we donate this hammer to a not-for-profit organization, is it still a hammer? After all, we didn't make a *profit* on it. The word *intending* may cover us, but still, shouldn't this word have a more detailed explanation? And who is *we*? Is it our entire organization or maybe just a subset? What does *profit* really mean anyway? Can two people read the word *profit* and see it very differently?

You see the problem. We need to think like a detective to find gaps and ambiguous statements in the text to make terms precise. After some debate, we update our **Product** definition to:

A product, also known as a finished product, is something that is in a state to be sold to a consumer. It has completed manufacturing, contains a wrapper, and is labeled for resale. A product is different than a raw material and a semi-finished good. A raw material, such as sugar or milk, or a semi-finished good, such as melted chocolate, is never sold to a consumer. If, in the future, sugar or milk is sold directly to consumers, then sugar and milk become products.

Examples:
Widgets Dark Chocolate 42 oz
Lemonizer 10 oz
Blueberry pickle juice 24 oz

Ask at least five people to see if they are all clear on this particular initiative's definition of a product. The best way to test precision is to try to break the definition. Think of lots of examples and see if everyone makes the same decision as to whether the examples are products or not.

In 1967, G.H. Mealy wrote a white paper where he made this statement:

We do not, it seems, have a very clear and commonly agreed upon set of notions about data—either what they are, how they should be fed and cared for, or their relation to the design of programming languages and operating systems.[10]

Although Mr. Mealy made this claim over 50 years ago, if we replace *programming languages and operating systems* with the word *databases*, we can make a similar claim today.

Aiming for precision can help us better understand our business terms and business requirements.

Minimal

The world around us is full of obstacles that can overwhelm our senses, making it very challenging to focus only on the relevant information needed to make intelligent decisions. Therefore, the model contains a minimal set of symbols and text, simplifying a subset of the real world by only including representations of what we need to understand. Much is filtered out on a model,

---

[10] G. H. Mealy, "Another Look at Data," AFIPS, pp. 525-534, 1967 Proceedings of the Fall Joint Computer Conference, 1967. http://tw.rpi.edu/media/2013/11/11/134fa/GHMealy-1967-FJCC-p525.pdf.

creating an incomplete but extremely useful reflection of reality. For example, we might need to communicate descriptive information about **Customer**, such as their name, birth date, and email address. However, we will not include information on the process of adding or deleting a customer.

Visuals

Visuals mean that we need a picture instead of lots of text. Our brains process images 60,000 times faster than text, and 90 percent of the information transmitted to the brain is visual.[11]

We might read an entire document but not reach that moment of clarity until we see a figure or picture summarizing everything. Imagine reading directions to navigate from one city to another versus the ease of reading a map that shows visually how the roads connect.

Three model components

The three components of a data model are entities, relationships, and attributes (including keys).

---

[11] https://www.t-sciences.com/news/humans-process-visual-data-better.

Entities

An entity is a collection of information about something important to the business. It is a noun considered basic and critical to your audience for a particular initiative. Basic means this entity is mentioned frequently in conversations while discussing the initiative. Critical means the initiative would be very different or non-existent without this entity.

The majority of entities are easy to identify and include nouns that are common across industries, such as **Customer, Employee**, and **Product**. Entities can have different names and meanings within departments, organizations, or industries based on audience and initiative (scope). An airline may call a **Customer** a *Passenger*, a hospital may call a **Customer** a *Patient*, an insurance company may call a **Customer** a *Policyholder*, yet they are all recipients of goods or services.

Each entity fits into one of six categories: who, what, when, where, why, or how. That is, each entity is either a who, what, when, where, why, or how. Table 3 contains a definition of each of these categories, along with examples.

Category	Definition	Examples
Who	Person or organization of interest to the initiative.	Employee, Patient, Player, Suspect, Customer, Vendor, Student, Passenger, Competitor, Author
What	Product or service of interest to the initiative. What the organization makes or provides that keeps it in business.	Product, Service, Raw Material, Finished Good, Course, Song, Photograph, Tax Preparation, Policy, Breed
When	Calendar or time interval of interest to the initiative.	Schedule, Semester, Fiscal Period, Duration
Where	Location of interest to the initiative. Location can refer to actual places as well as electronic places.	Employee Home Address, Distribution Point, Customer Website
Why	Event or transaction of interest to the initiative.	Order, Return, Complaint, Withdrawal, Payment, Trade, Claim
How	Documentation of the event of interest to the initiative. Records events such as a Purchase Order (a "How") recording an Order event (a "Why"). A document provides evidence that an event took place.	Invoice, Contract, Agreement, Purchase Order, Speeding Ticket, Packing Slip, Trade Confirmation

Table 3: Entity categories plus examples.

We traditionally show entities as rectangles on a data model, such as these two for our animal shelter:

Pet		Breed

Figure 17: Traditional entities.

Entity instances are the occurrences, examples, or representatives of that entity. The entity **Pet** may have multiple instances, such as Spot, Daisy, and Misty. The entity **Breed** may have multiple instances, such as German Shephard, Greyhound, and Beagle.

Entities and entity instances take on more precise names when discussing specific technologies. For example, entities are tables and instances are rows in a RDBMS like Oracle, and also in Cassandra.

Relationships

A relationship represents a business connection between two entities and traditionally appears on the model as a line connecting two rectangles. For example, here is a relationship between **Pet** and **Breed**:

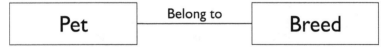

Figure 18: Relationship and label.

The phrase **Belong to** is called a *label*. A label adds meaning to the relationship. Instead of just saying that a **Pet** may relate to a **Breed**, we can say that a **Pet** may belong to a **Breed**. **Belong to** is more meaningful than **Relate**.

So far, we know that a relationship represents a business connection between two entities. It would be nice to know more about the relationship, such as whether a **Pet** may belong to more than one **Breed** or whether a **Breed** can categorize more than one **Pet**. Enter cardinality.

Cardinality means the additional symbols on the relationship line that communicate how many instances from one entity participate in the relationship with instances of the other entity.

There are several modeling notations, each with its own set of symbols. Throughout this book, we use a notation called *Information Engineering (IE)*. The IE notation has been a very popular notation since the early 1980s. If you use a notation other than IE within your organization, you must translate the following symbols into the corresponding symbols in your modeling notation.

We can choose any combination of zero, one, or many for cardinality. *Many* (some people use "more") means one or more. Yes, many includes one. Specifying one or many allows us to capture *how many* of a particular entity instance participate in a given relationship. Specifying zero or one allows us to capture whether an entity instance is or is not required in a relationship.

Recall this relationship between **Pet** and **Breed**:

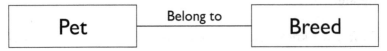

Figure 19: Relationship and label.

Let's now add cardinality.

We first ask the *Participation* questions to learn more. Participation questions tell us whether the relationship is 'one' or 'many'. So, for example:

- Can a **Pet** belong to more than one **Breed**?
- Can a **Breed** categorize more than one **Pet**?

A simple spreadsheet can keep track of these questions and their answers:

Question	Yes	No
Can a Pet belong to more than one Breed?		
Can a Breed categorize more than one Pet?		

We asked the animal shelter experts and received these answers:

Question	Yes	No
Can a Pet belong to more than one Breed?	✓	
Can a Breed categorize more than one Pet?	✓	

We learn that a **Pet** may belong to more than one **Breed**. For example, Daisy is part Beagle and part Terrier. We also learned that a **Breed** may categorize more than one **Pet**. Both Sparky and Spot are Greyhounds.

'Many' (meaning one or more) on a data model in the IE notation is a symbol that looks like a crow's foot (and is called a *crow's foot* by data folks). See Figure 20.

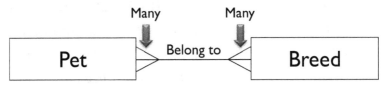

Figure 20: Displaying the answers to the Participation questions.

Now we know more about the relationship:

- Each **Pet** may belong to many **Breeds**.
- Each **Breed** may categorize many **Pets**.

We also always use the word 'each' when reading a relationship and start with the entity that makes the most sense to the reader, usually the one with the clearest relationship label.

This relationship is not yet precise, though. So, in addition to asking these two Participation questions, we also need to ask the *Existence* questions. Existence tells us for each relationship whether one entity can exist without the other term. For example:

- Can a **Pet** exist without a **Breed**?
- Can a **Breed** exist without a **Pet**?

We asked the animal shelter experts and received these answers:

Question	Yes	No
Can a Pet exist without a Breed?		✓
Can a Breed exist without a Pet?	✓	

So, we learn that a **Pet** cannot exist without a **Breed**, and that a **Breed** can exist without a **Pet**. This means, for example, that we may not have any Chihuahuas in our animal shelter. Yet we need to capture a **Breed** (and in this case, one or more **Breeds**) for every **Pet**. As soon as we know about Daisy, we need to identify at least one of her breeds, such as Beagle or Terrier.

Figure 21 displays the answers to these two questions.

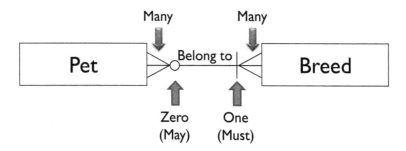

Figure 21: Displaying the answers to the Existence questions.

After adding existence, we have a precise relationship:

- Each **Pet** must belong to many **Breeds**.
- Each **Breed** may categorize many **Pets**.

The Existence questions are also known as the May/Must questions. When reading the relationship, the Existence questions tell us whether we say "may" or "must." A zero means "may", indicating optionality—the entity can exist without the other entity. A **Breed** *may* exist without a **Pet**, for example. A one means "must", indicating required—the entity cannot exist without the other entity. A **Pet** *must* belong to at least one **Breed**, for example.

We need to ask two more questions if we are working on the more detailed logical data model (which we discuss shortly). These are the *Identification* questions.

Identification tells us for each relationship whether one entity can be identified without the other term. For example:

- Can a **Pet** be identified without a **Breed**?
- Can a **Breed** be identified without a **Pet**?

We asked the animal shelter experts and received these answers:

Question	Yes	No
Can a Pet be identified without a Breed?	✓	
Can a Breed be identified without a Pet?	✓	

So, we learn that a **Pet** can be identified without knowing a **Breed**. We can identify the pet Sparky without knowing that Sparky is a German Shepherd. In addition, we can identify a **Breed** without knowing the **Pet**. This means, for example, that we can identify the Chihuahua breed without including any information from **Pet**.

A dotted line captures a non-identifying relationship. That is, when the answer to both questions is "yes". A solid line captures an identifying relationship. That is, when one of the answers is "no".

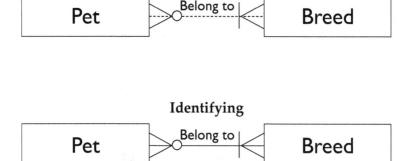

Figure 22: A non-identifying (top) and identifying (bottom) relationship.

So, to summarize, the Participation questions reveal whether each entity has a one or many relationship to the other entity. The Existence questions reveal whether each entity has an optional ("may") or mandatory ("must") relationship to the other entity. The Identification questions reveal whether each entity requires the other entity to bring back a unique entity instance.

Use instances to make things clear in the beginning and eventually help you explain your models to colleagues. See Figure 23 for an example.

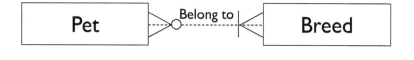

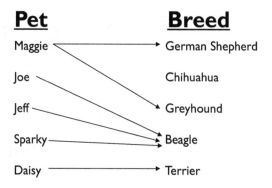

Figure 23: Use sample data to validate a relationship.

You can see from this dataset that a **Pet** can belong to more than one **Breed**, such as Maggie, which is a German Shepherd/Greyhound mix. You can also see that every **Pet** must belong to at least one **Breed**. We could also have a **Breed** that does not categorize any **Pets**, such as Chihuahua. In addition, a **Breed** can categorize multiple **Pets**, such as Joe, Jeff, and Sparky are all Beagles.

Answering all six questions leads to a precise relationship. Precise means we all read the model the same exact way.

Let's say that we have slightly different answers to our six questions:

Question	Yes	No
Can a Pet belong to more than one Breed?		✓
Can a Breed categorize more than one Pet?	✓	
Can a Pet exist without a Breed?		✓
Can a Breed exist without a Pet?	✓	
Can a Pet be identified without a Breed?	✓	
Can a Breed be identified without a Pet?	✓	

These six answers lead to this model:

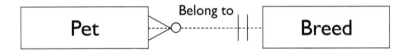

- Each **Pet** must belong to one **Breed**.
- Each **Breed** may categorize many **Pets**.

Figure 24: Different answers to the six questions lead to different cardinality.

This model only includes pure-breed pets, as a **Pet** must be assigned one **Breed**. No mutts in our shelter!

Be very clear on labels. Labels are the verbs that connect our entities (nouns). To read any complete sentence, we need both nouns and verbs. Make sure the labels on the relationship lines are as descriptive as possible. Here are some examples of good labels:

- Contain
- Provide
- Own
- Initiate
- Characterize

Avoid the following words as labels, as they provide no additional information to the reader. You can use these words in combination with other words to make a meaningful label; just avoid using these words by themselves:

- Have
- Associate
- Participate
- Relate
- Are

For example, replace the relationship sentence:

"Each **Pet** must *relate to* one **Breed**."

With:

"Each **Pet** must *belong to* one **Breed**."

Relationships take on more precise names when discussing specific technologies. For example, relationships are constraints in a RDBMS such as Oracle. There are not enforceable constraints in Cassandra. We manage relationships by storing the data in a denormalized table.

We can design the application to guarantee the consistency between different denormalized tables. We can execute data write operations to multiple tables simultaneously, and ensure that all replicas are kept up-to-date. This process improves query efficiency and read performance by allowing data to be retrieved quickly for each specific query type.

In addition to relationship lines, we can also have a subtyping relationship. The subtyping relationship groups common entities together. For example, we might group the **Dog** and **Cat** entities using subtyping under the more generic **Pet** term. In this example, we call **Pet** the grouping entity or supertype, and **Dog** and **Cat** would be the terms grouped together, also known as the subtypes, as shown in Figure 25.

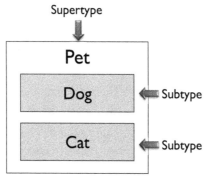

Figure 25: Subtyping is similar to the concept of inheritance.

We would read this model as:

- Each **Pet** may be either a **Dog** or a **Cat**.
- **Dog** is a **Pet**. **Cat** is a **Pet**.

The subtyping relationship means that all of the relationships (and attributes that we'll learn about shortly) that belong to the supertype from other terms also belong to each subtype. Therefore, the relationships to **Pet** also belong to **Dog** and **Cat**. So, for example, cats can be assigned breeds as well, so the relationship to **Breed** can exist at the **Pet** level instead of the **Dog** level, encompassing both cats and dogs. See Figure 26 for an example.

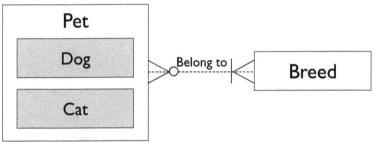

Figure 26: The relationship to Pet is inherited to Dog and Cat.

So, the relationship:

- Each **Pet** must belong to many **Breeds**.
- Each **Breed** may categorize many **Pets**.

Also applies to **Dog** and **Cat**:

- Each **Dog** must belong to many **Breeds**.
- Each **Breed** may categorize many **Dogs**.
- Each **Cat** must belong to many **Breeds**.
- Each **Breed** may categorize many **Cats**.

Not only does subtyping reduce redundancy, but it also makes it easier to communicate similarities across what would appear to be distinct and separate terms.

Attributes and keys

An entity contains attributes. An *attribute* is an individual piece of information whose values identify, describe, or measure instances of an entity. The entity **Pet** might contain the attributes **Pet Number** that identifies the **Pet**, **Pet Name** that describes the **Pet**, and **Pet Age** that measures the **Pet**.

Attributes take on more precise names when discussing specific technologies. For example, attributes are columns in a RDBMS such as Oracle, and also in Cassandra.

A candidate key is one or more attributes that uniquely identify an entity instance. We assign a **ISBN** (International Standard Book Number) to every title. The **ISBN** uniquely identifies each title and is, therefore, the title's candidate key. **Tax ID** can be a candidate key for an organization in some countries, such as the United States. **Account Code** can be a candidate key for an account. A **VIN** (Vehicle Identification Number) identifies a vehicle.

A candidate key must be unique and mandatory. Unique means a candidate key value must not identify more than one entity instance (or one real-world thing). Mandatory means a candidate key cannot be empty (also known as *nullable*). We must identify each entity instance by exactly one candidate key value.

The number of distinct values of a candidate key is always equal to the number of distinct entity instances. If the entity **Title** has **ISBN** as its candidate key, and if there are 500 title instances, there will also be 500 unique ISBNs.

Even though an entity may contain more than one candidate key, we can only select one candidate key as the primary key for an entity. A primary key is the candidate key chosen to be *the preferred* unique identifier for an entity. An alternate key is a candidate key that, although it has the properties of being unique and mandatory, was not chosen as the primary key. However, it may still be used to find specific entity instances.

The primary key appears above the line in the entity box, and the alternate key contains the 'AK' in parentheses. So, in the following **Pet** entity, **Pet Number** is the primary key and **Pet Name** is the alternate key. Having an alternate key on **Pet Name** means we cannot have two pets with the same name. Whether this can happen or not is a good discussion point. However, the model in its current state would not allow duplicate **Pet Names**.

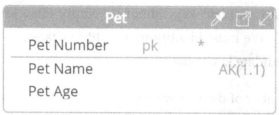

Figure 27: An alternate key on Pet Name means we cannot have two pets with the same name.

A candidate key can be either simple, compound, or composite. If it is simple, it can be either a business or surrogate key. Table 4 contains examples of each key type.

	SIMPLE	COMPOUND	COMPOSITE	OVERLOADED
BUSINESS	ISBN	PROMOTION TYPE CODE + PROMOTION START DATE	(CUSTOMER FIRST NAME + CUSTOMER LAST NAME + BIRTHDAY)	STUDENT GRADE
SURROGATE	BOOK ID			

Table 4: Examples of each key type.

Sometimes, a single attribute identifies an entity instance, such as **ISBN** for a title. When a single attribute makes up a key, we use the term *simple key*. A simple key can either be a business (also called natural) key or a surrogate key.

A business key is visible to the business (such as a **Policy Number** for a **Policy**). A surrogate key is never visible to the business. A technologist creates a surrogate key to help with a technology issue, such as space efficiency, speed, or integration. It is a unique identifier for a table, often a counter, usually fixed-size, and always system-generated without intelligence, so a surrogate key carries no business meaning.

Sometimes, it takes more than one attribute to uniquely identify an entity instance. For example, both a **Promotion Type Code** and **Promotion Start Date** may be necessary to identify a promotion. When more than one attribute makes up a key, we use the term *compound key*. Therefore, the **Promotion Type Code** and **Promotion Start Date** together are a compound candidate key for a promotion. When a key contains more than one piece of information, we use the term *composite key*. A simple key that includes the customer's first name, last name, and birthday, all in the same attribute, would be an example of a simple composite key. When a key contains different attributes, it is called an *overloaded* key. A **Student Grade** attribute might sometimes contain the actual grade, such as A, B, or C. At other times, it might just contain a P for Pass and F for Fail. **Student Grade**, therefore, would be an overloaded attribute. **Student Grade** sometimes contains the student's grade, and other times indicates whether the student has passed the class.

Let's look at the model in Figure 28.

Figure 28: The entity on the many sides contains a foreign key pointing back to the primary key from the entity on the one side.

Here are the rules captured on this model:

- Each **Gender** may categorize many **Pets**.
- Each **Pet** must be categorized by one **Gender**.
- Each **Pet** may Receive many **Vaccinations**.
- Each **Vaccination** may be given to many **Pets**.

The entity on the "one" side of the relationship is called the parent entity, and the entity on the "many" sides of the relationship is called the child entity. For example, in the relationship between **Gender** and **Pet**, **Gender** is the parent and **Pet** is the child. When we create a relationship from a parent entity to a child entity, the parent's primary key is copied as a foreign key to the child. You can see the foreign key, **Gender Code**, in the **Pet** entity.

A foreign key is one or more attributes that link to another entity (or, in the case of a recursive relationship where two instances of the same entity may be related, that is, a relationship that starts and ends with the same entity, a link to the same entity). At the physical level, a foreign key allows a relational database management system to navigate from one table to another. For example, if we need to know the **Gender** of a particular **Pet**, we can use the **Gender Code** foreign key in **Pet** to navigate to the parent **Gender**.

Three model levels

Traditionally, data modeling produces a set of structures for a Relational Database Management System (RDBMS). First, we build the Conceptual Data Model (CDM) (more appropriately called the Business Terms Model or BTM for short) to capture the common business language for the initiative (e.g., "What's a Customer?"). Next, we create the Logical Data Model (LDM) using the BTM's common business language to precisely define the business requirements (e.g., "I need to see the customer's name and address on this report."). Finally, in the Physical Data Model (PDM), we design these business requirements specific for a particular technology such as Oracle, Teradata, or SQL Server (e.g., "Customer Last Name is a variable length not null field with a non-unique index..."). Our PDM represents the RDBMS design for an application. We then generate the Data Definition Language (DDL) from the PDM, which we can run within a RDBMS environment to create the set of tables that will store the application's data. To summarize, we go from common business language to business requirements to design to tables.

Although the conceptual, logical, and physical data models have played a very important role in application development over the last 50 years, they will play an even more important role over the next 50 years.

Regardless of the technology, data complexity, or breadth of requirements, there will always be a need for a diagram that captures the business language (conceptual), the business requirements (logical), and the design (physical).

The names *conceptual, logical,* and *physical,* however, are deeply rooted in the RDBMS side. Therefore, we need more encompassing names to accommodate both RDBMS and NoSQL for all three levels.

Align = Conceptual, Refine = Logical, Design = Physical

Using the terms Align, Refine, and Design instead of Conceptual, Logical, and Physical has two benefits: greater purpose and broader context.

Greater purpose means that by rebranding into Align, Refine, and Design, we include what the level does in the name. Align is about agreeing on the common business vocabulary so everyone is *aligned* on terminology and general initiative scope. Refine is about capturing the business requirements. That is, refining our knowledge of the initiative to focus on what is important. Design is about the technical requirements. That is, ensuring we accommodate the unique software and hardware needs on our model.

A broader context means there is more than just the models. When we use terms such as conceptual, most project teams only see the model as the deliverable and do not recognize all of the work that went into producing the model or other related deliverables such as definitions, issue/question resolutions, and lineage (lineage meaning where the data comes from). The align phase includes the conceptual (business terms) model, the refine phase includes the logical model, and the design phase includes the physical model. We don't lose our modeling terms. Instead, we distinguish the model from its broader phase. For example, instead of saying we are in the logical data modeling phase, we say we are in the refine phase, where the logical data model is one of the deliverables. The logical data model exists within the context of the broader refine phase.

However, suppose you are working with a group of stakeholders who may not warm up to the traditional names of conceptual, logical, and physical. In that case, you can call the conceptual the *alignment model,* the logical the *refinement model,* and the physical the *design model.* Use the terms that would have the largest positive impact on your audience.

The conceptual level is Align, the logical Refine, and the physical Design. Align, Refine, and Design—easy to remember and even rhymes!

Business terms (Align)

We have had many experiences where people who need to speak a common business language do not consistently use the same set of terms. For example, Steve recently facilitated a discussion between a senior business analyst and a senior manager at a large insurance company.

The senior manager expressed his frustration on how a business analyst was slowing down the development of his business analytics application. "The team was meeting with the product owner and business users to complete the user stories on insurance quotes for our upcoming analytics application on quotes, when a business analyst asked the question, *What is a quote?* The rest of the meeting was wasted on trying to answer this question. Why couldn't we just focus on getting the Quote Analytics requirements, which we were in that meeting to do? We are supposed to be Agile!"

If there was a lengthy discussion trying to clarify the meaning of a quote, there is a good chance this insurance company does not understand a quote well. All business users may agree that a quote is an estimate for a policy premium but disagree at what point an estimate becomes a quote. For example, does an estimate have to be based on a certain percentage of facts before it can be considered a quote?

How well will Quote Analytics meet the user requirements if the users are not clear as to what a *quote* is? Imagine needing to know the answer to this question:

How many life insurance quotes were written last quarter in the northeast?

Without a common alignment and understanding of *quote*, one user can answer this question based on their definition of *quote*, and someone else can answer based on their different definition of *quote*. One of these users (or possibly both) will most likely get the wrong answer.

Steve worked with a university whose employees could not agree on what a *student* meant, a manufacturing company whose sales and accounting departments differed on the meaning of *return on total assets*, and a financial company whose analysts battled relentlessly over the meaning of a *trade*—it's all the same challenge we need to overcome, isn't it?

It's about working towards a common business language.

A common business language is a prerequisite for success in any initiative. We can capture and communicate the terms underlying business processes and requirements, enabling people with different backgrounds and roles to understand and communicate with each other.

A Conceptual Data Model (CDM), more appropriately called a Business Terms Model (BTM), is a language of symbols and text that simplifies an informational landscape by providing a precise, minimal, and visual tool scoped for a particular initiative and tailored for a particular audience.

This definition includes the need to be well-scoped, precise, minimal, and visual. Knowing the type of visual that will have the greatest effectiveness requires knowing the audience for the model.

The audience includes the people who will validate and use the model. Validate means telling us whether the model is correct or needs adjustments. Use means reading and benefiting from the model. The scope encompasses an initiative, such as an application development project or a business intelligence program.

Knowing the audience and scope helps us decide which terms to model, what the terms mean, how the terms relate to each other, and the most beneficial type of visual. Additionally, knowing the scope ensures you don't "boil the ocean" and model every possible term in the enterprise. Instead, only focus on those that will add value to your current initiative.

Although this model is traditionally called a *conceptual data model*, the term "conceptual" is often not received as a very positive term by those outside the data field. "Conceptual" sounds like a term the IT team would come up with. Therefore, we prefer to call the "conceptual data model" the "business terms model" and will use this term going forward. It is about business terms, and including the term "business" raises its importance as a business-focused deliverable and also aligns with data governance.

A business terms model often fits nicely on a single piece of paper—and not a plotter-size paper! Limiting a BTM to one page is important because it encourages us to select only key terms. We can fit 20 terms on one page but not 500 terms.

Being well-scoped, precise, minimal, and visual, the BTM provides a common business language. As a result, we can capture and communicate complex and encompassing business processes and requirements, enabling people with different backgrounds and roles to initially discuss and debate terms, and to eventually communicate effectively using these terms.

With more and more data being created and used, combined with intense competition, strict regulations, and rapid-spread social media, the financial, liability, and credibility stakes have never been higher. Therefore, the need for a common business language has never been greater. For example, Figure 29 contains a BTM for our animal shelter.

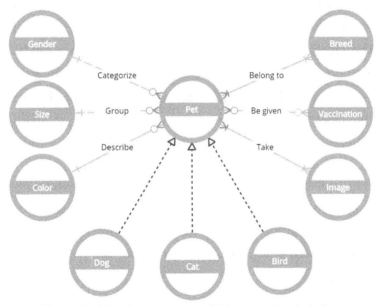

Figure 29: A business terms model for our animal shelter.

Each of these entities will have a precise and clear definition. For example, **Pet** might have a similar definition to what appears in Wikipedia:

A pet, or companion animal, is an animal kept primarily for a person's company or entertainment rather than as a working animal, livestock, or a laboratory animal.

More than likely, though, there will be something about the definition that provides more meaning to the reader of a particular data model and is more specific to a particular initiative, such as:

A pet is a dog, cat, or bird that has passed all the exams required to secure adoption. For example, if Sparky has passed all of his physical and behavioral exams, we would consider Sparky a pet. However, if Sparky has failed at least one exam, we will label Sparky an animal that we will reevaluate later.

Let's now walk through the relationships:

- Each Pet may be either a Dog, Cat, or Bird.
- Dog is a Pet.
- Cat is a Pet.
- Bird is a Pet.
- Each Gender may categorize many Pets.
- Each Pet must be categorized by one Gender.
- Each Size may group many Pets.
- Each Pet must be grouped by one Size.
- Each Color may describe many Pets.
- Each Pet must be described by one Color.
- Each Pet must belong to many Breeds.
- Each Breed may categorize many Pets.
- Each Pet may be given many Vaccinations.

- Each Vaccination may be given to many Pets.
- Each Pet must take many Images.
- Each Image must be taken of many Pets.

Logical (Refine)

A logical data model (LDM) is a business solution to a business problem. It is how the modeler refines the business requirements without complicating the model with implementation concerns such as software and hardware.

For example, after capturing the common business language for a new order application on a BTM, the LDM will refine this model with attributes and more detailed relationships and entities to capture the requirements for this order application. The BTM would contain definitions for **Order** and **Customer**, and the LDM would contain the **Order** and **Customer** attributes needed to deliver the requirements. Returning to our animal shelter example, Figure 30 contains a subset of the logical data model for our animal shelter.

Figure 30: Logical data model subset for our animal shelter.

The requirements for our shelter application appear on this model. This model shows the attributes and relationships needed to deliver a solution to the business. For example, in the **Pet** entity, each **Pet** is identified by a **Pet Number** and described by its name and gender. **Gender** and **Vaccination** are defined lists. We also capture that a **Pet** must have one **Gender** and can receive any number (including zero) of **Vaccinations**.

Note that a LDM in the context of relational databases respects the rules of normalization. Hence, in the above diagram, there are associative entities, also known as "junction tables", which prepare for the physical implementation of many-to-many relationships.

Since Cassandra allows us to denormalize, we often don't need these "junction tables" and opt for a simpler view of the same business rules. We can keep together what belongs together, following the Domain-Driven Design concept of "aggregates" discussed below, and leveraging denormalization. See Figure 31.

An important part of the requirements-gathering exercise is identifying, quantifying, and qualifying the workload by recording frequency of queries, latency of results, volume and velocity of data, retentions, etc. This is discussed in more detail in the Refine chapter.

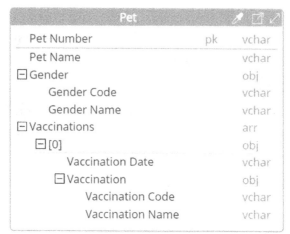

Figure 31: This denormalized representation can easily lead to a normalized physical data model, whereas the opposite is not necessarily true in more complex configurations.

Domain-Driven Design

It is useful at this stage to briefly cover a popular methodology used in software development: Domain-Driven Design. Its principles have some relevance in the context of data modeling for NoSQL.

Eric Evans is the author of the book, *Domain-Driven Design: Tackling Complexity in the Heart of Software,* published in 2003, which is considered one of the most influential works on Domain-Driven Design (DDD). Its principles include:

- **Ubiquitous language**: establishing a common language used by all project stakeholders, and reflecting the concepts and terms relevant to the business.

- **Bounded context**: managing the complexity of the system by breaking it down into smaller, more manageable pieces. This is done by defining a boundary around each specific domain of the software system. Each bounded context has its own model and language that is appropriate for that context.

- **Domain model**: using a business terms model of the domain that represents the important entities, their relationships, and the behaviors of the domain.

- **Context mapping**: defining and managing the interactions and relationships between different bounded contexts. Context mapping helps to ensure that different models are consistent with each other and that communication between teams is effective.

- **Aggregates**: identifying clusters of related objects and treating each of them as a single unit of change. Aggregates help to enforce consistency and integrity within a domain.

- **Continuous refinement**: an iterative process with continuous refinement of the domain model as new insights and requirements are discovered. The domain model should evolve and improve over time based on feedback from stakeholders and users.

These principles are striking by common sense and applicable to enhance data modeling. Yet, the nuances are important. For example, we have seen that a BTM helps build a common vocabulary. DDD pushes further for developers to use this language in the code and the name of collections/tables and fields/columns.

Some data modeling traditionalists have expressed reservations about DDD (and also about Agile development.) For every methodology and technology, there are, of course, examples of misinterpretation and misguided efforts. But applied with clairvoyance and experience, DDD and Agile can lead to great success. We see DDD principles as directly applicable to data modeling to further enhance its relevance rather than as an opposite approach.

DDD is particularly relevant in the context of NoSQL databases and modern architecture patterns and stacks, including event-driven and micro-services. Specifically, the DDD concept of "aggregates" matches the hierarchical nature of collections with nested objects and denormalization. As a result, the strict definition of a logical data model is too constraining as it implies that the technology-agnostic model respects the rules of normalization. Hackolade has extended the capabilities of its technology-agnostic models to allow complex data types for nesting and denormalization to accommodate the support of NoSQL structures.

Physical (Design)

The physical data model (PDM) is the logical data model compromised for specific software or hardware. The BTM captures our common business vocabulary, the LDM our business requirements, and the PDM our technical requirements. That is, the PDM is a data model of our business requirements structured to work well with our technology. The physical represents the technical design.

While building the PDM, we address the issues that have to do with specific hardware or software, such as, how can we best design our structures to:

- Process this operational data as quickly as possible?
- Make this information secure?
- Answer these business questions with a sub-second response?

For example, Figure 32 contains a relational version and Figure 33 a nested version of a subset of the physical data model for our animal shelter:

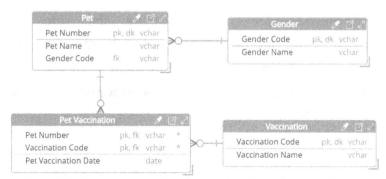

Figure 32: Relational physical data models for our animal shelter.

pet_by_type			
type	pk,PK	text	*
gendercode	pk,CK, ↑	integer	*
petid	pk,CK, ↓	uuid	*
name		text	
age		integer	
gendername		text	
⊟vaccinations		list<udt>	
⊟ [0] vaccination		udt	
code		integer	
date		dt	
name		text	

Figure 33: Nested physical data models for our animal shelter.

We have compromised our logical model to work with specific technology. For example, if we are implementing in a RDBMS such as Oracle, we might need to combine (denormalize) structures together to make retrieval performance acceptable.

Figure 32 is a normalized RDBMS model and Figure 33 shows one possible denormalization approach in Cassandra. Information belonging together stays together with using list and User Defined Type. We replace the cardinality of the relational junction table **Pet Vaccination** with an array to store multiple **Vaccinations**. This aggregation approach enables the referential integrity of the atomic unit of each document. Note that the nesting does not prevent the existence of a **Vaccination** table if an access pattern in the application requires it, but we would then require synchronization of the denormalized data to ensure consistency.

Three model perspectives

Relational Database Management System (RDBMS) and NoSQL are the two main modeling perspectives. Within the RDBMS, the two settings are relational and dimensional. Within NoSQL, the one setting is query. Therefore, the three modeling perspectives are relational, dimensional, and query.

Table 5 contrasts relational, dimensional, and query. In this section, we will go into more detail into each of these perspectives.

A RDBMS stores data in sets based on Ted Codd's groundbreaking white papers written from 1969 through 1974. Codd's ideas were implemented in the RDBMS with tables (entities at the physical level) containing attributes. Each table has a primary key and foreign key constraints to enforce the relationships between tables. The RDBMS has been around for so many years primarily because of its ability to retain data integrity by enforcing rules that maintain high-quality data. Secondly, the RDBMS enables storing data efficiency, reducing redundancy, and saving storage space at the cost of using more CPU power. Over the last decade, the benefit of saving space has diminished as disks get cheaper while CPU performance is not improving. Both trajectories favor NoSQL databases these days.

Factor	Relational	Dimensional	Query
Benefit	Precisely representing data through sets	Precisely representing how data will be analyzed	Precisely representing how data will be received and accessed
Focus	Business rules *constraining* a business process	Business questions *analyzing* a business process	Access paths *providing insights* into a business process
Use case	Operational (OLTP)	Analytics (OLAP)	Discovery
Parent perspective	RDBMS	RDBMS	NoSQL
Example	A Customer must own at least one Account.	How much revenue did we generate in fees by Date, Region, and Product? Also want to see by Month and Year…	Which customers own a checking account that generated over $10,000 in fees this year, own at least one cat, and live within 500 miles of New York City?

Table 5: Comparing relational, dimensional, and query.

NoSQL means "NoRDBMS". A NoSQL database stores data differently than a RDBMS. A RDBMS stores data in tables (sets) where primary and foreign keys drive data integrity and navigation. A NoSQL database does not store data in sets. For example, Cassandra uses a data storage format optimized for its distributed architecture and high availability characteristics. It uses a combination of concepts, including partitions, rows, and columns, to efficiently organize and store denormalized data. Other NoSQL solutions may store data in Resource Description Framework (RDF) triples, Extensible Markup Language (XML), or JavaScript Object Notation (JSON).

Relational, dimensional, and query can exist at all three model levels, giving us nine different types of models, as shown in Table 6. We discussed the three levels of Align, Refine, and Design in the previous section. We align on a common business language, refine our business requirements, and then design our database. For example, if we are modeling a new claims application for an insurance company, we might create a relational model capturing the business rules within the claims process. The BTM would capture the claims business vocabulary, the LDM would capture the claims business requirements, and the PDM would capture the claims database design.

	RELATIONAL	DIMENSIONAL	NoSQL
BUSINESS TERMS (ALIGN)	TERMS AND RULES	TERMS AND PATHS	TERMS AND QUERIES
LOGICAL (REFINE)	SETS	MEASURES WITH CONTEXT	QUERY-FOCUSED HIERARCHY
PHYSICAL (DESIGN)	COMPROMISED SETS	STAR SCHEMA OR SNOWFLAKE	ENHANCED HIERARCHY

Table 6: Nine different types of models.

Relational

Relational models work best when there is a requirement to capture and enforce business rules. For example, a relational model may be ideal if an operational application requires applying many business rules, such as an order application ensuring that every order line belongs to one and only one order, and that each order line is identified by its order number plus a sequence number. The relational perspective focuses on business rules.

We can build a relational model at all three levels: business terms, logical, and physical. The relational business terms model contains the common business language for a particular initiative. Relationships capture the business rules between these terms. The relational logical data model includes entities along with their definitions, relationships, and attributes. The relational physical data model includes physical structures such as tables, columns, and constraints. The business terms, logical, and physical data models shared earlier are examples of relational. See Figure 34, Figure 35, and Figure 36.

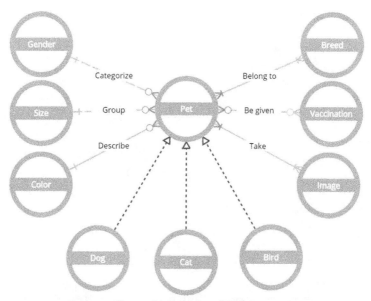

Figure 34: Relational BTM.

Figure 35: Relational LDM.

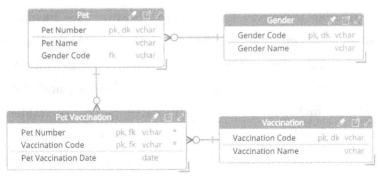

Figure 36: Relational PDM.

Figure 37 contains another example of a BTM.

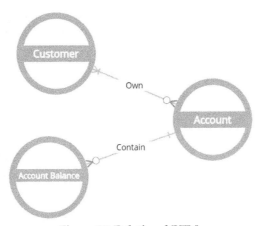

Figure 37: Relational BTM.

The relationships capture that:

- Each **Customer** may own many **Accounts**.
- Each **Account** must be owned by many **Customers**.
- Each **Account** may contain many **Account Balances**.
- Each **Account Balance** must belong to one **Account**.

We wrote the following definitions during one of our meetings with the project sponsor:

Customer	A customer is a person or organization who has opened one or more accounts with our bank. If each member of a household has their own account, each member of a household is considered a distinct customer. If someone has opened and closed an account, they are still considered a customer.
Account	An account is a contractual arrangement by which our bank holds funds on behalf of a customer.
Account Balance	An account balance is a financial record of how much money a customer has in a particular account with our bank at the end of a given time period, such as someone's checking account balance at the end of a month.

For the relational logical data model, we assign attributes to entities (sets) using a set of rules called *normalization*.

Although normalization has a foundation in mathematics (set theory and predicate calculus), we see it more as a technique to design a flexible structure. More specifically, we define normalization as a process of asking business questions, increasing your knowledge of the business and enabling you to build flexible structures that support high-quality data.

The business questions are organized around levels, including First Normal Form (1NF), Second Normal Form (2NF), and Third Normal Form (3NF). William Kent has neatly summarized these three levels:

Every attribute depends upon the key, the whole key, and nothing but the key, so help me Codd.

"Every attribute depends upon the key" is 1NF, "the whole key" is 2NF, and "nothing but the key" is 3NF. Note that the higher levels of normalization include the lower levels, so 2NF includes 1NF, and 3NF includes 2NF and 1NF.

To make sure that every attribute depends upon the key (1NF), we need to make sure for a given primary key value, we get at most one value back from each attribute. For example, **Author Name** assigned to a **Book** entity would violate 1NF because for a given book, such as this book, we can have more than author. Therefore, **Author Name** does not belong to the **Book** set (entity), and we move it to a different entity. More than likely, we assign **Author Name** to the **Author** entity, and a relationship will exist between **Book** and **Author,** stating among other things, that a **Book** can be written by more than one **Author.**

To make sure every attribute depends upon the whole key (2NF), we need to make sure we have the minimal primary key. For example, if the primary key for a **Book** is both **ISBN** and a **Book Title**, we would quickly learn that **Book Title** is not necessary to have in the primary key. An attribute such as **Book Price** would depend directly on the **ISBN**. Therefore, including **Book Title** in the primary key would not add value.

To make sure there are no hidden dependencies ("nothing but the key," which is 3NF), we need to make sure every attribute depends directly on the primary key and nothing else. For example, the attribute **Order Gross Amount** does not depend directly on the primary key of **Order** (most likely, **Order Number**). Instead, **Order Gross Amount** depends upon **List Price** and **Item Quantity,** which we use to derive the **Order Gross Amount.**

Data Modeling Made Simple, by Steve Hoberman, goes into more detail into each of the levels of normalization, including the levels above 3NF. Realize the main purpose of normalization is to correctly organize attributes into sets. Also, note that we build the normalized model according to the properties of the data and not according to how the stakeholders use the data.

Dimensional models are built to easily answer specific business questions, and NoSQL models are built to answer queries and easily identify patterns. The relational model is the only one focused on the data's intrinsic properties and not usage.

Dimensional

A dimensional data model captures the business *questions* behind one or more business processes. The answers to the questions are metrics, such as **Gross Sales Amount** and **Customer Count**.

A dimensional model is a data model whose only purpose is to allow efficient and user-friendly filtering, sorting, and summing of measures. That is, analytics applications. The relationships on a dimensional model represent navigation paths instead of business rules, as with the relational model. The scope of a dimensional model is a collection of related measures plus context that together address some business process. We build dimensional models based on one or more business questions that evaluate a business process. We parse the business questions into measures and ways of looking at these measures to create the model.

For example, suppose we work for a bank and would like to better understand the fee generation process. In that case, we might ask the business question, "What is the total amount of fees received by **Account Type** (such as Checking or Savings), **Month, Customer Category** (such as Individual or Corporate), and **Branch**?" See Figure 38. This model also communicates the requirement to see fees not just at a **Month** level but also at a **Year** level, not just a **Branch** level, but also at a **Region** and **District** level.

You might encounter terms such as **Year** and **Month** which are commonly understood terms, and therefore minimal time can be invested in writing a definition. Make sure, though, that these are commonly understood terms, as sometimes even **Year** can have multiple meanings, such as whether the reference is to a fiscal or standard calendar.

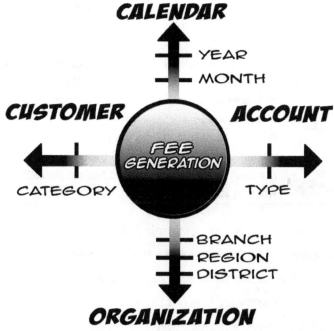

Figure 38: A dimensional BTM for a bank.

Term definitions:

Fee Generation	Fee generation is the business process in which money is charged to customers for the privilege to conduct transactions against their account, or money charged based on time intervals, such as monthly charges to keep a checking account open with a low balance.
Branch	A branch is a physical location open for business. Customers visit branches to conduct transactions.
Region	A region is our bank's own definition of dividing a country into smaller pieces for branch assignment or reporting purposes.
District	A district is a grouping of regions used for organizational assignments or reporting purposes. Districts, such as North America and Europe, can and often do cross country boundaries.
Customer Category	A customer category is a grouping of one or more customers for reporting or organizational purposes. Examples of customer categories are Individual, Corporate, and Joint.
Account Type	An account type is a grouping of one or more accounts for reporting or organizational purposes. Examples of account types are Checking, Savings, and Brokerage.
Year	A year is a period of time containing 365 days, consistent with the Gregorian calendar.
Month	A month is each of the twelve named periods into which a year is divided.

Fee Generation is an example of a meter. A meter represents the business process that we need to measure. The meter is so important to the dimensional model that the name of the meter is often the name of the application: the **Sales** meter, the Sales Analytics Application. **District,**

Region, and **Branch** represent the levels of detail we can navigate within the **Organization** dimension. A *dimension* is a subject whose purpose is to add meaning to the measures. For example, **Year** and **Month** represent the levels of detail we can navigate within the **Calendar** dimension. So, this model contains four dimensions: **Organization, Calendar, Customer**, and **Account**.

Suppose an organization builds an analytical application, such as a sales analytics application, to answer questions on how a business process performs. Business questions become very important in this case, so we build a dimensional data model. The dimensional perspective focuses on business questions. We can build a dimensional data model at all three levels: business terms, logical, and physical. Figure 38 displays our business terms model, Figure 39 shows the logical, and Figure 40 the physical.

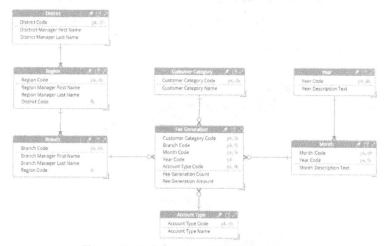

Figure 39: A dimensional LDM for a bank.

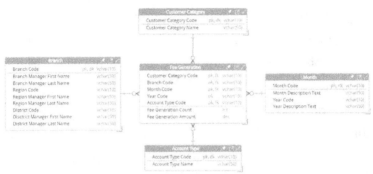

Figure 40: A dimensional PDM for a bank.

Query

Suppose an organization builds an application to discover something new about a business process, such as a fraud detection application. Queries become very important in that case, so we build a query data model. We can build a query data model at all three levels: business terms, logical, and physical. Figure 41 contains a query business terms model, the query logical data models, and the query physical data model.

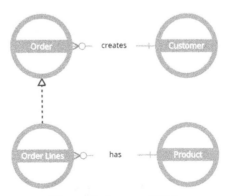

Figure 41: A query BTM.

The Query BTM does not look any different from other BTMs as the vocabulary and scope are the same, independent of the physical database implementation. In fact, we can even ask the Participation and Existence questions for each relationship in our query BTM, if we feel that it would add value. In the above example:

- a **Customer** creates an **Order**
- an **Order** is made of **Order Lines**
- an **Order Line** has a **Product**

It is possible to toggle the display of attributes for the different entities.

When it comes to the data model, however, access patterns and workload analysis dictate the model.

If we would need to get the orders by **order_id** and need all the details of the order and customer, we could prepare the table in Figure 42.

The first logical model could lead to a single table in Cassandra. In contrast, it will, most likely, be normalized into three tables when instantiated to a physical model for a relational database. If the access pattern needs to get the data by filtering customer, we can prepare a table as shown in Figure 43.

We demonstrate denormalization in Figure 43 because it is very common in Cassandra to duplicate data across different tables. It is possible to access by using **cust_id** and **order_id**, by using **order_id** as the clustering key. **Order_id** could also be used in range queries.

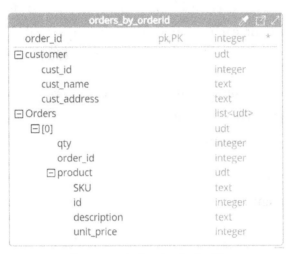

Figure 42: Orders by Order Id

orders_by_customer_id			
cust_id	pk,PK	integer	*
order_id	pk,CK, ↑	integer	*
cust_name		text	
cust_address		text	
qty		integer	
orderid		integer	
SKU		text	
product_id		integer	
product_desc		text	
unit_price		integer	

Figure 43: Orders by Customer Id

CHAPTER 1

Align

This chapter will explain the data modeling align phase. We explain the purpose of aligning our business vocabulary, introduce our animal shelter case study, and then walk through the align approach. We end this chapter with three tips and three takeaways.

Purpose

The align stage aims to capture a common business vocabulary within a business terms model for a particular initiative.

For NoSQL models, you might use a different term than a business terms model, such as a *query alignment model*. We also like this term, which is more specific to the purpose of a NoSQL BTM, as our goal is modeling the queries.

Our animal shelter

A small animal shelter needs our help. They currently advertise their ready-to-adopt pets on their own website. They use a Microsoft Access relational database to keep track of their animals, and they publish this data weekly on their website. See Figure 44 for their current process.

A Microsoft Access record is created for each animal after the animal passes a series of intake tests and is deemed ready for adoption. The animal is called a pet once it is ready for adoption.

Once a week, a shelter employee updates the pet records on the shelter's website. New pets are added, and adopted pets are removed.

Figure 44: Animal shelter current architecture.

Not many people know about this shelter, and, therefore, animals often remain unadopted for much longer than the national average. Consequently, they would like to partner with a group of animal shelters to form a consortium where all of the shelters' pet information will appear on a much more popular website. Our shelter will need to extract data from its current MS Access database and send it to the consortium database in JSON format. Next, the consortium will load these JSON feeds into their Cassandra database with a web front end.

The animal shelter built the business terms model (BTM) in Figure 45 to capture the common business language for the initiative.

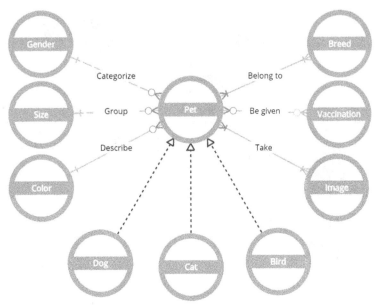

Figure 45: Animal shelter BTM.

In addition to this diagram, the BTM also contains precise definitions for each term, such as this definition of **Pet** mentioned earlier in the chapter:

A pet is a dog, cat, or bird that has passed all the exams required to secure adoption. For example, if Sparky has passed all of his physical and behavioral exams, we would consider Sparky a pet. However, if Sparky has failed at least one exam, we will label Sparky an animal that we will reevaluate later.

Our animal shelter knows its world well and has built fairly solid models. Recall they will send a subset of their data to a consortium, which the consortium's Cassandra database will receive and load for display on their website. Let's go through the align, refine, and design approach for the consortium, and then work on the data structure required to move the shelter's data from Microsoft Access to Cassandra.

Approach

The align stage is about developing the initiative's common business vocabulary. We will follow the steps shown in Figure 46.

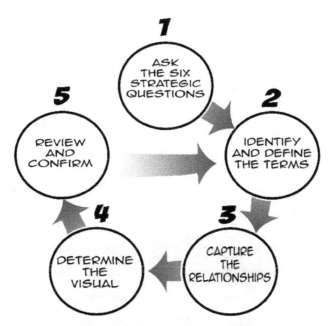

Figure 46: Steps to create a BTM.

Before you begin any project, we must ask six strategic questions (Step 1). These questions are a prerequisite to the success of any initiative because they ensure we choose the right terms for our BTM. Next, identify all terms within the scope of the initiative (Step 2). Make sure each term is clearly and completely defined. Then, determine how these terms are related to each other (Step 3). Often, you will need to go back to Step 2 at this point because in capturing relationships, you may come up with new terms. Next, determine the most beneficial visual for your audience (Step 4). Consider the visual that would resonate best with those needing to review and use your BTM. As a final step, seek approval of your BTM (Step 5). At this point, there are often additional changes to the model, and we cycle through these steps until the model is accepted.

Let's build a BTM following these five steps.

Step 1: Ask the six strategic questions

We need to ask six questions to ensure a valuable BTM. These questions appear in Figure 47.

1. **What is our initiative?** This question ensures we know enough about the initiative to determine the scope. Knowing the scope lets us decide which terms should appear on the initiative's BTM. In his book Domain-Driven Design, Eric Evans introduces the concept of "Bounded Context," which is all about understanding and defining your

scope. For example, terms such as **Animal**, **Shelter Employee**, and **Pet Food** are out of scope.

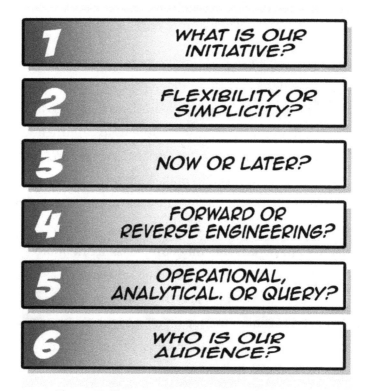

1	*WHAT IS OUR INITIATIVE?*
2	*FLEXIBILITY OR SIMPLICITY?*
3	*NOW OR LATER?*
4	*FORWARD OR REVERSE ENGINEERING?*
5	*OPERATIONAL, ANALYTICAL, OR QUERY?*
6	*WHO IS OUR AUDIENCE?*

Figure 47: Six questions to ensure model success.

2. **Flexibility or simplicity?** This question ensures we introduce generic terms only if there is a need for flexibility. Generic terms allow us to accommodate new types of terms that we do not know about today and also allow us to better group similar terms together. For example, **Person** is flexible and **Employee** is simple. **Person** can include other terms we have not yet considered, such as **Adopter,**

Veterinarian, and **Volunteer.** However, **Person** can be a more difficult term to relate to than **Employee.** We often describe our processes using business-specific terms like **Employee.**

3. **Now or later?** This question ensures we have chosen the correct time perspective for our BTM. BTMs capture a common business language at a point in time. Suppose we intend to capture how business processes work or are analyzed today. In that case, we need to make sure terms, along with their definitions and relationships, reflect a current perspective (now). Suppose we are intent on capturing how business processes work or are analyzed at some point in the future, such as one year or three years into the future. In that case, we need to make sure terms, along with their definitions and relationships, reflect a future perspective (later).

4. **Forward or reverse engineering?** This question ensures we select the most appropriate "language" for the BTM. If business requirements drive the initiative, then it is a forward engineering effort and we choose a business language. It does not matter whether the organization is using SAP or Siebel, the BTM will contain business terms. If an application is driving the initiative, then it is a reverse engineering effort and we choose an

application language. If the application uses the term **Object** for the term **Product**, it will appear as **Object** on the model and be defined according to how the application defines the term, not how the business defines the term. As another example of reverse engineering, you might have some type of physical data structure as your starting point, such as a database layout, or an XML or JSON document. For example, the following JSON snippet might reveal the importance of **Shelter Volunteer** as a business term:

```
{
  "name": "John Smith",
  "age": 35,
  "address": {
    "street": "123 Main St",
    "city": "Anytown",
    "state": "CA",
    "zip": "12345"
  }
}
```

5. **Operational, analytics, or query?** This question ensures we choose the right type of BTM—relational, dimensional, or query. Each initiative requires its respective BTM.

6. **Who is our audience?** We need to know who will review our model (validator) and who will use our model going forward (users).

1. What is our initiative?

Mary is the animal shelter volunteer responsible for intake. Intake is the process of receiving an animal and preparing the animal for adoption. She has been a volunteer for over ten years, and was the main business resource in building the original Microsoft Access database.

She is enthusiastic about the new initiative, seeing it as a way to get animals adopted in less time. We might start by interviewing Mary, where the goal is to have a clear understanding of the initiative, including its scope:

> **You**: Thanks for making time to meet with me. This is just our first meeting, and I don't want to keep you behind our allocated time, so let's get right to the purpose of our interview and then a few questions. The earlier we identify our scope and then define the terms within this scope, the greater the chance for success. Can you please share with me more about this initiative?

> **Mary**: Sure! The main driver for our initiative is to make our furry friends get adopted faster. Today, on average, our pets are adopted in two weeks. We and other small local shelters would like to get this down to five days on average. Maybe even less, hope so. We will send our pet data to a consortium we have formed with other local shelters to centralize our listings and reach a wider audience.

> **You**: Do you have all types of pets, or just dogs and cats?

Mary: I'm not sure what kinds of pets the other shelters have other than dogs and cats, but we also have birds up for adoption.

You: Ok, and are there any pets to exclude from this initiative?

Mary: Well, it takes a few days to assess an animal to determine whether it is ready for adoption. We run some tests and sometimes procedures. I like to use the term pet when an animal has completed these processes and is now ready for adoption. So, we do have animals that are not yet pets. We are only including pets in this initiative.

You: Got it. And when somebody is looking for a furry best friend, what kinds of filters would they use?

Mary: I've talked with volunteers at the other shelters, too. We feel after filtering first on the type of pet, such as dog, cat, or bird, filtering by breed, gender, color, and size would be the most important filters.

You: What kinds of information would someone expect to see when clicking on a pet description returned by the filter selections?

Mary: Lots of images, a cute name, maybe information on the pet's color or breed. That sort of thing.

You: Makes sense. What about people? Do you care about people as part of this initiative?

Mary: What do you mean?

You: Well, the people who drop off pets and the people who adopt pets.

Mary: Yes, yes. We keep track of this information. By the way, the people who drop off animals we call surrenderers and the people who adopt pets are adopters. We are not sending any person details to the consortium. We don't see it relevant and don't want to risk getting sued over privacy issues. Spot the dog will never sue us, but Bob the surrenderer might.

You: I can understand that. Well, I think I understand the scope of the initiative, thank you.

We now have a good understanding of the scope of the initiative. It includes all pets (not all animals) and no people. As we refine the terminology, we might have more questions for Mary about scope.

2. Flexibility or simplicity?

Let's continue the interview to answer the next question.

You: Flexibility or simplicity?

Mary: I don't understand the question.

You: We need to determine whether to use generic terms or, for lack of a better word, more concrete terms. Using generic terms, such as mammal instead of dog or cat, allows us to accommodate future terms later, such as other kinds of mammals like monkeys or whales.

Mary: We haven't had many whales up for adoption this month. [laughs]

You: Ha!

Mary: Flexibility sounds appealing, but we shouldn't go overboard. We might eventually have other kinds of pets, so a certain level of flexibility would be useful here. But not too much. I remember working on the Microsoft Access system, and someone was trying to get us to use a Party concept to capture dogs and cats. It was too hard for us to get our heads around it. Too fuzzy, if you know what I mean.

You: I do know what you mean. Ok, a little flexibility to accommodate different kinds of pets, but not to go overboard. Got it.

3. Now or later?

Now on to the next question.

You: Should our model reflect how things are now at the shelter or how you would like it to be after the consortium's application is live?

Mary: I don't think it matters. We are not changing anything with the new system. A pet is a pet.

You: Ok, that makes things easy.

As we can see from our conversations on these first three questions, getting to the answers is rarely straightforward and easy. However, it is much more efficient to ask them at the beginning of the initiative instead of making assumptions early on and performing rework later, when changes are time-consuming and expensive.

4. Forward or reverse engineering?

Since we first need to understand how the business works before implementing a software solution, this is a forward engineering project, and we will choose the forward engineering option. This means driven by requirements and, therefore, our terms will be business terms instead of application terms.

5. Operational, analytics, or query?

Since this initiative is about displaying pet information to drive pet adoption, which is query, we will build a query BTM.

6. Who is our audience?

That is, who is going to validate the model and who is going to use it going forward? Mary seems like the best candidate to be the validator. She knows the existing application and processes very well and is vested in ensuring the new initiative succeeds. Potential adopters will be the users of the system.

Step 2: Identify and define the terms

We first focus on the user stories, then determine the detailed queries for each story, and finally sequence these queries in the order they occur. It can be iterative. For example, we might identify the sequence between two queries and realize that a query in the middle is missing, which will require modifying or adding a user story. Let's go through each of these three steps.

1. Write user stories

User stories have been around for a long time and are extremely useful for NoSQL modeling. Wikipedia defines a user story as: *…an informal, natural language description of features of a software system.*

The user story provides the scope and overview for the BTM, also known as a query alignment model. A query alignment model accommodates one or more user stories. The purpose of a user story is to capture at a very high level how an initiative will deliver business value. User stories take the structure of the template in Figure 48.

TEMPLATE	COVERS
AS A (STAKEHOLDER)	WHO?
I WANT TO (REQUIREMENT)	WHAT?
SO THAT (MOTIVATION)	WHY?

Figure 48: User story template.

Here are some examples of user stories from tech.gsa.gov:

- As a Content Owner, I want to be able to create product content so that I can provide information and market to customers.

- As an Editor, I want to review content before it is published so that I can ensure it is optimized with correct grammar and tone.

- As a HR Manager, I need to view a candidate's status so that I can manage their application process throughout the recruiting phases.

- As a Marketing Data Analyst, I need to run the Salesforce and Google analytics reports so that I can build the monthly media campaign plans.

To keep our animal shelter example relatively simple, assume our animal shelter and others that are part of the consortium met and determined these are the most popular user stories:

1. As a potential dog adopter, I want to find available dogs for adoption.

2. As a potential dog adopter, I want to find a particular breed and gender that I am looking for.

3. As a potential dog adopter, I want to find a particular color and gender that I am looking for.

2. Application Workflow (Capturing queries)

Next, we capture the queries for the one or more user stories within our initiative's scope. While we want to capture multiple user stories to ensure we have a firm grasp of the scope, having just a single user story that drives a NoSQL application is ok. A query starts off with a "verb" and is an action to do something. Some NoSQL database vendors use the phrase "access pattern" instead of query. We will use the term "query" to also encompass "access pattern". Here are the queries that satisfy our three user stories:

Q1: Only show pets available for adoption.

Q2: Search available dogs by availability, breed, and gender.

Q3: Search available dogs by availability, breed, and color.

Q4: Search available dogs by availability, color, and gender.

Now that we have direction, we can work with the business experts to identify and define the terms within the initiative's scope. Recall our definition of a term as a noun that represents a collection of business data and is considered both basic and critical to your audience for a particular initiative. A term can fit into one of six categories: who, what, when, where, why, or how. We can use these six categories to create a terms template for capturing the terms on our BTM. See Figure 49.

WHO ?	WHAT ?	WHEN ?	WHERE ?	WHY ?	HOW ?

Figure 49: Terms template.

We meet again with Mary and came up with this completed template in Figure 50, based on our queries.

WHO ?	WHAT ?	WHEN ?	WHERE ?	WHY ?	HOW ?
SURRENDERER	PET	VACCINATION DATE	CRATE	VACCINATE	VACCINATION
ADOPTER	DOG			ADOPT	ADOPTION
	CAT			PROMOTE	PROMOTION
	BIRD				
	BREED				
	GENDER				
	COLOR				
	SIZE				
	IMAGE				

Figure 50: Initially completed template for our animal shelter.

Notice that this is a brainstorming session, and terms might appear on this template but not on the relational BTM. Excluded terms fit into three categories:

- **Too detailed**. Attributes will appear on the LDM and not the BTM. For example, **Vaccination Date** is more detailed than **Pet** and **Breed**.

- **Out of scope**. Brainstorming is a great way to test the scope of the initiative. Often, terms added to the terms template require additional discussions to determine whether they are in scope. For example, **Surrenderer** and **Adopter** we know are out of scope for the animal shelter's initiative.

- **Redundancies**. Why and How can be very similar. For example, the event **Vaccinate** is documented by the **Vaccination**. The event **Adopt** is documented by **Adoption**. Therefore, we may not need both the event and documentation. In this case, we choose the documentation. That is, we choose How instead of Why.

After taking a lunch break, we met again with Mary and refined our terms template, as shown in Figure 51.

We might have a lot of questions during this brainstorming session. It is a great idea to ask questions as they come up.

WHO?	WHAT?	WHEN?	WHERE?	WHY?	HOW?
~~SURRENDERER~~	PET	~~VACCINATION DATE~~	~~CRATE~~	~~VACCINATE~~	VACCINATION
~~ADOPTER~~	DOG			~~ADOPT~~	~~ADOPTION~~
	CAT			~~PROMOTE~~	~~PROMOTION~~
	BIRD				
	BREED				
	GENDER				
	COLOR				
	SIZE				
	IMAGE				

Figure 51: Refined template for our animal shelter.

There are three benefits of raising questions:

- **Become known as the detective**. Become comfortable with the level of detective work needed to arrive at a precise set of terms. Look for holes in the definition where ambiguity can sneak in, and ask questions, the answers to which will make the definition precise. Consider the question, "Can a pet be of more than one breed?" The answer to this question will refine how the consortium views pets, breeds, and their relationship. A skilled detective remains pragmatic as well, careful to avoid "analysis paralysis". A skilled data modeler must also be pragmatic to ensure the delivery of value to the project team.

- **Uncover hidden terms**. Often the answers to questions lead to more terms on our BTM—terms that we might have missed otherwise. For example, better understanding the relationship between **Vaccination** and **Pet** might lead to more terms on our BTM.

- **Better now than later**. The resulting BTM offers a lot of value, yet the process of getting to that final model is also valuable. Debates and questions challenge people, make them rethink, and, in some cases, defend their perspectives. If questions are not raised and answered during the process of building the BTM, the questions will be raised and need to be addressed later on in the lifecycle of the initiative, often in the form of data and process surprises, when changes are time-consuming and expensive. Even simple questions like "Are there other attributes we could use to describe a pet?" can lead to a healthy debate, resulting in a more precise BTM.

Here are definitions for each term:

Pet	A dog, cat, or bird that is ready and available to be adopted. An animal becomes a pet after passing certain exams our shelter staff administers.

Gender	The biological sex of the pet. There are three values that we use at the shelter: • Male • Female • Unknown The unknown value is when we are unsure of the gender.
Size	The size is most relevant for dogs, and there are three values that we assign at the shelter: • Small • Medium • Large Cats and birds are assigned medium, except for kittens, which are assigned small, and parrots, which are large.
Color	The primary shade of the pet's fur, feathers, or coat. Examples of colors include brown, red, gold, cream, and black. If a pet has multiple colors, we either assign a primary color or assign a more general term to encompass multiple colors, such as textured, spotted, or patched.
Breed	From Wikipedia, because this definition applies to our initiative: *A breed is a specific group of domestic animals having homogeneous appearance, homogeneous behavior, and/or other characteristics that distinguish it from other organisms of the same species.*
Vaccina -tion	A shot given to a pet to protect it from disease. Examples of vaccinations are rabies for dogs and cats, and polyomavirus vaccine for birds.
Image	A photograph taken of the pet that will be posted on the website.

Dog	From Wikipedia, because this definition applies to our initiative: *The dog is a domesticated descendant of the wolf. Also called the domestic dog, it is derived from the extinct Pleistocene wolf, and the modern wolf is the dog's nearest living relative. Dogs were the first species to be domesticated by hunter-gatherers over 15,000 years ago before the development of agriculture.*
Cat	From Wikipedia, because this definition applies to our initiative: *The cat is a domestic species of small carnivorous mammal. It is the only domesticated species in the family Felidae and is commonly referred to as the domestic cat or house cat to distinguish it from the wild members of the family.*
Bird	From Wikipedia, because this definition applies to our initiative: *Birds are a group of warm-blooded vertebrates constituting the class Aves, characterized by feathers, toothless beaked jaws, the laying of hard-shelled eggs, a high metabolic rate, a four-chambered heart, and a strong yet lightweight skeleton.*

Step 3: Capture the relationships

Even though this is a query BTM, we can ask the Participation and Existence questions to precisely display the business rules for each relationship. Participation questions determine whether there is a one or a many symbols on the relationship line next to each term. Existence questions determine whether there is a zero (may) or one (must) symbol on the relationship line next to either term.

Working with Mary, we identify these relationships in the model:

- **Pet** can be a **Bird, Cat,** or **Dog.** (Subtyping)
- **Pet** and **Image.**
- **Pet** and **Breed.**
- **Pet** and **Gender.**
- **Pet** and **Color.**
- **Pet** and **Vaccination.**
- **Pet** and **Size.**

Table 7 contains the answers to the Participation and Existence questions for each of these seven relationships (excluding the subtyping relationship). After translating the answer to each question into the model, we have the animal shelter BTM in Figure 52.

Question	Yes	No
Can a Gender categorize more than one Pet?	✓	
Can a Pet be categorized by more than one Gender?		✓
Can a Gender exist without a Pet?	✓	
Can a Pet exist without a Gender?		✓
Can a Size categorize more than one Pet?	✓	
Can a Pet be categorized by more than one Size?		✓
Can a Size exist without a Pet?	✓	
Can a Pet exist without a Size?		✓
Can a Color describe more than one Pet?	✓	
Can a Pet be described by more than one Color?		✓
Can a Color exist without a Pet?	✓	
Can a Pet exist without a Color?		✓

Question	Yes	No
Can a Pet be described by more than one Breed?	✓	
Can a Breed describe more than one Pet?	✓	
Can a Pet exist without a Breed?		✓
Can a Breed exist without a Pet?	✓	
Can a Pet be given more than one Vaccination?	✓	
Can a Vaccination be given to more than one Pet?	✓	
Can a Pet exist without a Vaccination?	✓	
Can a Vaccination exist without a Pet?	✓	
Can a Pet take more than one Image?	✓	
Can an Image be taken of more than one Pet?	✓	
Can a Pet exist without an Image?		✓
Can an Image exist without a Pet?		✓

Table 7: Answers to the Participation and Existence questions.

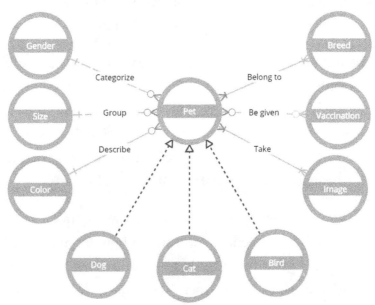

Figure 52: Our animal shelter BTM (showing rules).

These relationships are read as:

- Each **Gender** may categorize many **Pets**.
- Each **Pet** must be categorized by one **Gender**.
- Each **Size** may group many **Pets**.
- Each **Pet** must be grouped by one **Size**.
- Each **Color** may describe many **Pets**.
- Each **Pet** must be described by one **Color**.
- Each **Pet** must belong to many **Breeds**.
- Each **Breed** may be assigned to many **Pets**.
- Each **Pet** may be given many **Vaccinations**.
- Each **Vaccination** may be given to many **Pets**.
- Each **Pet** must take many **Images**.
- Each **Image** must be taken of many **Pets**.
- Each **Pet** may either be a **Dog, Cat,** or **Bird**.
- **Dog** is a **Pet**. **Cat** is a **Pet**. **Bird** is a **Pet**.

The answers to the participation and existence questions are context-dependent. That is, the scope of the initiative determines the answers. In this case, because our scope is the subset of the animal shelter's business we will use as part of this consortium's project, we know at this point that we must describe a **Pet** by only one **Color**.

We know, though, that we will use a Cassandra database to answer these queries. You can see how the traditional data model provides value in terms of making us ask the right questions and then providing a powerful communication medium showing the terms and their business rules. Even if we are not implementing our solution in a relational database, this BTM provides value.

Build a relational data model even though the solution is in a NoSQL database such as Cassandra, if you feel there can be value. That is, if you feel there is value in explaining the terms with precision along with their business rules, build the relational BTM. If you feel there is value in organizing the attributes into sets using normalization, build the relational LDM. It will help you organize your thoughts and provide you with a very effective communication tool.

Our end goal, though, is to create a Cassandra database. Therefore, we need a query BTM. So, we need to determine the order in which someone would run the queries.

Graphing the sequence of queries leads to the query BTM. The query BTM is a numbered list of all queries necessary to deliver the user stories within the initiative's scope. The model also shows a sequence or dependency among the queries. The query BTM for our five queries would look like what appears in Figure 53.

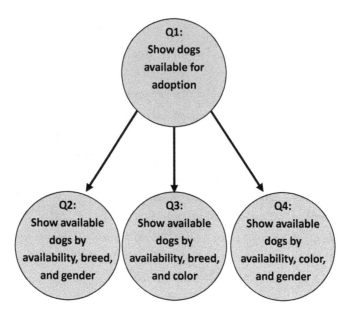

Figure 53: Our animal shelter BTM (showing queries).

All of the queries depend on the first query. That is, we first need to filter by animal type.

Step 4: Determine the visual

Someone will need to review your work and use your model as input for future deliverables such as software development, so deciding on the most useful visual is an important step. After getting an answer to Strategic Question #4, *Who is our audience?*, we know that Mary will be our validator.

There are many different ways of displaying the BTM. Factors include the technical competence of the audience and the existing tools environment.

However, it would be helpful to know which data modeling notations and data modeling tools the organization currently uses. If the audience is familiar with a particular data modeling notation—such as Information Engineering (IE), which we have been using throughout this book—that is the notation we should use. If the audience is familiar with a particular data modeling tool, such as IDERA's ER/Studio, erwin DM, or Hackolade Studio, and that data modeling tool uses a different notation, we should use that tool with that notation to create the BTM.

Luckily, the two BTMs we created, one for rules and one for queries, are very intuitive, so there is a very good chance our models will be well-understood by the audience.

Step 5: Review and confirm

Previously, we identified the person or group responsible for validating the model. Now, we need to show them the model and make sure it is correct. Often, after reviewing the model at this stage, we make some changes and then show them the model again. This iterative cycle continues until the validator approves the model.

Three tips

1. **Organization.** The steps you went through in building this "model" are the same steps we go through in building any model. It is all about organizing information. Data modelers are fantastic organizers. We take the chaotic real world and show it in a precise form, creating powerful communication tools.

2. **80/20 Rule.** Don't go for perfection. Too many requirements meetings end with unfulfilled goals by spending too much time discussing a minute particular issue. After a few minutes of discussion, if you feel the issue's discussion may take up too much time and not lead to a resolution, document the issue and keep going. You will find that for modeling to work well with Agile and other iterative approaches, you may have to forego perfection and sometimes even completion. Much better to document the unanswered questions and issues and keep going. Much better to deliver something imperfect yet still very valuable than deliver nothing. You will find that you can get the data model about 80% complete in 20% of the time. One of your deliverables will be a document containing

unanswered questions and unresolved issues. Once we resolve all of these issues and questions, which will take about 80% of your time to complete, the model will be 100% complete.

3. **Diplomat.** As William Kent said in **Data and Reality** (1978), *so, once again, if we are going to have a database about books, before we can know what one representative stands for, we had better have a consensus among all users as to what "one book" is.* Invest time trying to get consensus on terms before building a solution. Imagine someone querying on pets without having a clear definition of what a pet is.

Three takeaways

1. Six strategic questions must be asked before you begin any project (Step 1). These questions are a prerequisite to the success of any initiative because they ensure we choose the right terms for our BTM. Next, identify all terms within the scope of the initiative (Step 2). Make sure each term is clearly and completely defined. Then determine how these terms are related (Step 3). Often, you will need to go back to Step 2 at this point, because in capturing relationships, you may come up with new terms. Next, determine the most beneficial visual for your audience (Step 4). Consider the visual that would

resonate best with those needing to review and use your BTM. As a final step, seek approval of your BTM (Step 5). Often, at this point, there are additional changes to the model, and we cycle through these steps until the model is accepted.

2. Create a relational BTM in addition to a query BTM if you feel there would be value in capturing and explaining the participation and existence rules.

3. Never underestimate the value of precise and complete definitions.

CHAPTER 2

Refine

This chapter will explain the data modeling refine phase. We explain the purpose of refine, refine the model for our animal shelter case study, and then walk through the refine approach. We end the chapter with three tips and three takeaways.

Purpose

The purpose of the refinement stage is to create the logical data model (LDM) based on our common business vocabulary defined during the align stage. Refine is how the modeler captures the business requirements without complicating the model with implementation concerns, such as software and hardware.

The shelter's Logical Data Model (LDM) uses the common business language from the BTM to precisely define the business requirements. The LDM is fully-attributed yet independent of technology. We build the relational LDM by normalizing, which we covered in Chapter 1. Figure 54 contains the shelter's relational LDM.

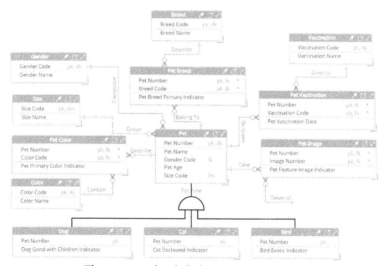

Figure 54: Animal shelter relational LDM.

This model does not change based on requirements. Therefore, we can use it as the starting point model for all queries. Let's briefly walk through the model. The shelter identifies each **Pet** with a **Pet Number**, which is a unique counter assigned to the **Pet** the day the **Pet** arrives. Also entered at this time are the pet's name (**Pet Name**) and age (**Pet Age**). If the **Pet** does not have a name, it is given one by the shelter employee entering the pet's information. If the age is unknown, the shelter employee estimates the age while entering the pet's information. If the **Pet** is a **Dog,** the shelter employee entering the information performs a few assessments to determine whether the Dog is good with children (**Dog Good With Children Indicator**). If the **Pet** is a **Cat**, the shelter employee determines whether the **Cat** has been declawed (**Cat Declawed Indicator**). If the Pet is a **Bird**, the shelter employee enters whether it is an exotic bird such as a parrot (**Bird Exotic Indicator**).

Approach

The refine stage is all about determining the business requirements for the initiative. The end goal is a logical data model which captures the attributes and relationships needed to answer the queries. The steps to complete appear in Figure 55.

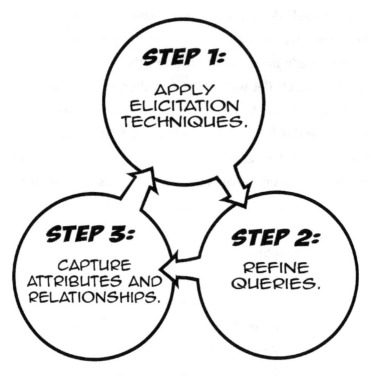

Figure 55: Refinement steps.

Similar to determining the more detailed structures in a traditional logical data model, we determine the more detailed structures needed to deliver the queries during the refinement stage. You can, therefore, call the query LDM a query refinement model if you prefer. The query refinement model is all about discovery and captures the answers to the queries that reveal insights into a business process.

Step 1: Apply elicitation techniques

This is where we interact with the business stakeholders to identify the attributes and relationships needed to answer the queries. We keep refining, usually until we run out of time. Techniques we can use include interviewing, artifact analysis (studying existing or proposed business or technical documents), job shadowing (watching someone work), and prototyping. You can use any combination of these techniques to obtain the attributes and relationships to answer the queries. Often, these techniques are used within an Agile framework. You choose which techniques to use based on your starting point and the needs of the stakeholders. For example, if a stakeholder says, "I don't know what I want, but I'll know when I see it," building a prototype might be the best approach.

Analyze workloads

An important part of this exercise is to identify, quantify, and qualify the workload.

You need to identify each operation as either a read or a write operation, and understand the read-to-write ratio. Make a list of all Create, Read, Update, and Delete (CRUD) operations, and take the time to go through the exercise of drawing wireframes of screens and reports, and of assembling workflow diagrams. Thinking these through and validating them with subject matter experts will inevitably reveal facts you might have previously overlooked.

For write operations, you want to know for how long to hold data, the frequency by which the system receives data, average document size, retention, and durability. Start your design exercise with the most critical operation and work your way down the list.

For read operations, you also want to document the patterns and required freshness of the data, taking into account eventual consistency and read latency. Data freshness is related to replication time if you read from a secondary, or to the acceptable time for a piece of data derived from other pieces. It defines how fast written data must be accessible for read operations: immediately (data consistent at all times), within 10 milliseconds, 1 second, 1 minute, 1 hour, or 1 day. For example, reading the top reviews associated with a product, cached in the product document, may have a tolerated 1-day freshness. Read latency is specified in milliseconds, where p95 and p99 values represent the 95th and 99th percentile values (a read latency p95 value of 100ms means that 95 out of 100 requests took 100ms or less to complete).

This information helps validate the choice of design pattern, orients the necessary indexes, and impacts the sizing and provisioning of the hardware, hence the budget for the project. Different data modeling patterns impact read performance, number of write operations, cost of indexes, etc. So, you may have to make compromises and balance sometimes contradictory needs.

You may use a spreadsheet or any other method to document the results of your workload analysis, based on the example in Figure 56 and built into Hackolade Studio for Cassandra. When considering schema evolution later in the lifecycle, you will be able to review the values originally recorded, as reality might be very different than what was initially estimated. Document the query predicates with the specific expression and parameters used to determine which documents should be retrieved. Several other data points in the form in Figure 56 deserve some clarification.

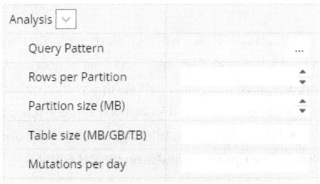

Figure 56: Workload analysis data capture screen.

Step 2: Refine queries

The refinement process is iterative, and we keep refining, again, usually until we run out of time.

Step 3: Capture attributes and relationships

Ideally, because of the hierarchical nature of document (and also key-value) databases, we should strive to answer one or more queries with a single structure. Although this might seem "anti-normalization", one structure organized to a particular query is much faster and simpler than connecting multiple structures. The logical data model contains the attributes and related structures needed for each of the queries identified in the query refinement model.

Using artifact analysis, we can start with the animal shelter's logical and use this model as a good way to capture the attributes and relationships within our scope. Based on the queries, we do not need quite a few of our concepts for searching or filtering, so they can become additional descriptive attributes on the **Pet** entity.

For example, no critical queries involved vaccinations. Therefore, we can simplify this model subset from the model in Figure 57 to the model in Figure 58.

Figure 57: Normalized model subset.

Figure 58: Denormalized model subset.

This example illustrates how traditional RDBMS models differ from NoSQL. In our original logical model, it was important to communicate that a **Pet** can receive many **Vaccinations** and a **Vaccination** can be given to many **Pets**. In NoSQL, however, since there were no queries needing to filter or search by vaccination, the vaccination attributes just become other descriptive attributes of **Pet**. The **Vaccination Code** and **Vaccination Name** attributes are now a nested array within **Pet**. So, for example, if Spot the Dog had five vaccinations, they would all be listed within Spot's record. Following this same logic, the pet's colors and images also become nested arrays, as shown in Figure 59.

In addition, to help with querying, we need to create a **Pet Type** structure instead of the Dog, Cat, and Bird subtypes. After determining the available pets for adoption, we need to distinguish whether the **Pet** is a **Dog, Cat,** or **Bird**. Our model would now look like what appears in Figure 60.

In addition to the denormalization seen before, this example illustrates the polymorphic nature of Cassandra as an alternative to the inheritance tables of relational databases. This single schema describes and can validate different document types for dogs, cats, and birds, in addition to the common structure. Relational subtyping is accomplished here with the one of choice, which allows multiple subschemas.

Junction tables found in relational models are replaced here by arrays of subobjects, the list data type allowing for an ordered list of items.

Figure 59: Nested arrays added for color and images.

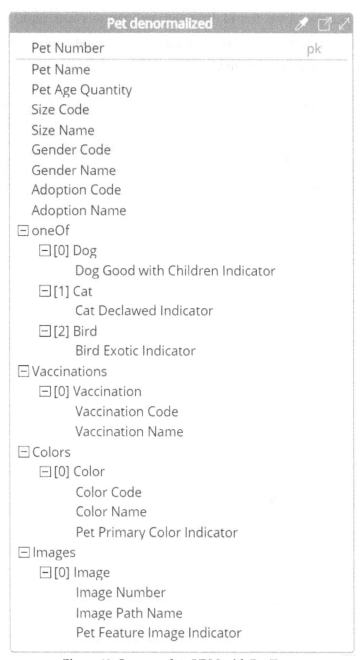

Figure 60: Our complete LDM with Pet Type.

Three tips

1. **Access patterns:** the query-driven approach is critical to leverage the benefits of NoSQL when creating an LDM. Don't be tempted by old normalization habits unless the workload analysis reveals relationship cardinality that warrants normalization.

2. **Aggregates:** keep together what belongs together! A nested structure in a single document can ensure atomicity and consistency of inserts, updates, and queries without expensive joins. It is also beneficial for developers who are used to working with objects, and it is easier to understand for humans.

3. **It is easier to normalize a denormalized structure than the opposite:** a normalized LDM is not technology-agnostic if it includes junction tables. Or it is "technology-agnostic" only if your physical targets are exclusively relational and don't include NoSQL. A denormalized LDM, on the other hand, can be easily normalized for relational physical targets by a good data modeling tool, while providing denormalized structures based on the access patterns identified earlier.

Three takeaways

1. The purpose of the refinement stage is to create the logical data model (LDM) based on our common business vocabulary, defined for our initiative during the align stage. Refine is how the modeler captures the business requirements without complicating the model with implementation concerns, such as software and hardware.

2. An LDM is typically fully attributed yet independent of technology. But today, this strict definition is being challenged because technology targets can differ in nature: relational databases, the different families of NoSQL, storage formats for data lakes, APIs, etc.

3. It used to be, with relational databases, that you wanted to design a structure that could handle any possible future query that might be run down the road. With NoSQL, you want to design schemas that are specific, not only for an application but for each access pattern (write or read) in that application.

Chapter 3

Design

This chapter will explain the data modeling design phase. We explain the purpose of design, design the model for our animal shelter case study, and then walk through the design approach. We end the chapter with three tips and three takeaways.

Purpose

The purpose of the design stage is to create the physical data model (PDM) based on the business requirements defined in our logical data model. Design is how the modeler captures the technical requirements without compromising the business requirements, yet accommodating the initiative's software and technology needs used for the initiative.

The design stage is also where we accommodate history. That is, we modify our structures to capture how data changes over time. For example, the Design stage would allow us to keep track of not just the most recent name for a pet but also the original. For example, the animal shelter changes a pet's name from Sparky to Daisy. Our design could store the original pet's name and the most current one, so we would know Daisy's original name was Sparky. Although this is not a book on temporal data or modeling approaches that gracefully allow for storing high data volatility or varying history requirements, such as the Data Vault,[12] you would need to consider such factors in the Design stage.

Figure 61 shows the Physical Data Model (PDM) of the animal shelter's Microsoft Access database design.

---

[12] For more on the data vault, read John Giles' *The Elephant in the Fridge*.

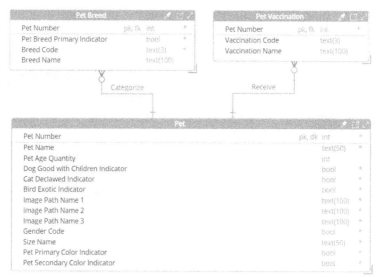

Figure 61: PDM of the shelter's Access database.

Note that the PDM includes formatting and nullability. Also, this model is heavily denormalized. For example:

- Although the logical communicates that a **Pet** can have any number of images, their design only allows up to three images for each **Pet**. The shelter uses **Image_Path_Name_1** for the featured image.

- Notice how we address the decode entities from the logical. We denormalize the one-to-many relationships into **Pet**. **Gender_Name** is not needed because everyone knows the codes. People are not familiar with **Size_Code,** so we only store **Size_Name**. We denormalize **Breed** into **Pet_Breed**. It is common for decode entities to be

modeled in different ways on the physical,
depending on the requirements.

- We denormalize **Vaccination** into **Pet_Vaccination**.

For Cassandra, it would change depending on how the
application will access the table. See Figure 62.

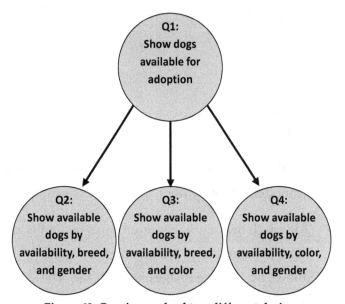

Figure 62: Queries can lead to a different design.

Let's check some examples:

For Query 1, show only the dogs available for adoption:

*Select * from pet_by_type_breed_gender where type='Dog' and
availability='A';*

Even though we have more columns like *breed* and *gender*
code as a clustering key in the primary key as shown in

Figure 63, we can just select the partition key *(pet_type and availability) without using the clustering keys.* This way, we can use the same table in Figure 63 for Q1 and Q2.

pet_by_type_breed_gender			
pet_type	pk,PK	text	*
availability	pk,PK	text	*
breed_code	pk,CK, ↑	text	*
pet_gendercode	pk,CK, ↑	integer	*
pet_id		uuid	
pet_name		text	
pet_age		integer	
size_name		text	
pet_breed_primary_indicator		bool	
breed name		text	
pet_primary_color		text	
pet_secondary_color		text	
⊟ vaccinations		list<udt>	
⊟ [0] vaccination		udt	
code		integer	
date		dt	
name		text	
⊟ image_paths		set<str>	
[0] image_path		text	
dog_good_with_children_indicator		bool	
cat_declawed_indicator		bool	
bird_exotic_indicator		bool	

Figure 63: PDM for Query 1.

For Query 2, search for available dogs by availability, breed, and gender using the same table in Figure 63 and Figure 64:

```
Select * from pet_by_type_breed_gender where
type='Dog' and availability='A' and
breed_code='Labrador Retriever' and
pet_gender_code='F';
```

pet_by_type_breed_gender			
pet_type	pk,PK	text	*
availability	pk,PK	text	*
breed_code	pk,CK, ↑	text	*
pet_gendercode	pk,CK, ↑	integer	*
pet_id		uuid	
pet_name		text	
pet_age		integer	
size_name		text	
pet_breed_primary_indicator		bool	
breed name		text	
pet_primary_color		text	
pet_secondary_color		text	
⊟vaccinations		list<udt>	
⊟[0] vaccination		udt	
code		integer	
date		dt	
name		text	
⊟image_paths		set<str>	
[0] image_path		text	
dog_good_with_children_indicator		bool	
cat_declawed_indicator		bool	
bird_exotic_indicator		bool	

Figure 64: PDM for Query 2.

For Query 3, search for available dogs by availability, breed, and color:

```
Select * from pet_by_type_breed_color where
type='Dog' and availability='A' and
breed_code='Labrador Retriever' and
pet_primary_color in ('Black','Chocolate');
```

pet_by_type_breed_color			
pet_type	pk,PK	text	*
availability	pk,PK	text	*
breed_code	pk,CK, ↑	text	*
pet_primary_color	pk,CK, ↑	text	*
pet_id		uuid	
pet_name		text	
pet_gendercode		integer	
pet_age		integer	
size_name		text	
pet_breed_primary_indicator		bool	
breed name		text	
pet_secondary_color		text	
⊟ vaccinations		list<udt>	
⊟ [0] vaccination		udt	
code		integer	
date		dt	
name		text	
⊟ image_paths		set<str>	
[0] image_path		text	
dog_good_with_children_indicator		bool	
cat_declawed_indicator		bool	
bird_exotic_indicator		bool	

Figure 65: PDM for Query 3.

For Query 4, search for available dogs by availability, color, and gender:

```
Select * from pet_by_type_color_gender where
type='Dog' and availability='A' and
pet_gendercode='M' and pet_primary_color
in('Black','Chocolate');
```

pet_by_type_color_gender			
pet_type	pk,PK	text	*
availability	pk,PK	text	*
pet_primary_color	pk,CK, ↑	text	*
pet_gendercode	pk,CK, ↑	integer	*
pet_id		uuid	
pet_name		text	
pet_age		integer	
size_name		text	
pet_breed_primary_indicator		bool	
breed_code		text	
breed name		text	
pet_secondary_color		text	
⊟ vaccinations		list<udt>	
⊟ [0] vaccination		udt	
code		integer	
date		dt	
name		text	
⊟ image_paths		set<str>	
[0] image_path		text	
dog_good_with_children_indicator		bool	
cat_declawed_indicator		bool	
bird_exotic_indicator		bool	

Figure 66: PDM for Query 4.

Approach

The design stage is all about developing the database-specific design for the initiative. The end goal is the query PDM, which we can also call the *query design model*. For our animal shelter initiative, this model captures the Cassandra design. The steps to complete appear in Figure 67.

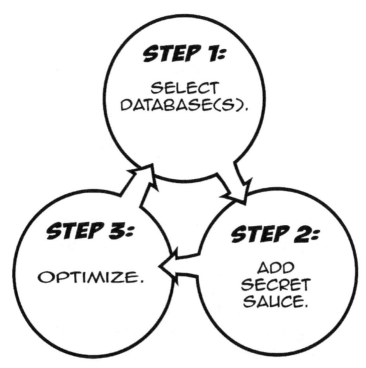

Figure 67: Design steps.

Step 1: Select database(s)

We now know enough to decide which database would be ideal for the application. Sometimes, we might choose multiple databases if we feel it would be the best architecture for the application. We know in the consortium's case that they are using JSON for transport and Cassandra for storage.

Step 2: Add secret sauce

Cassandra data modeling patterns

Denormalizing

As we have seen earlier, you will not be able to use JOIN with Cassandra tables. Denormalization will be your best friend as a data modeling technique, meaning data might be repeated across multiple tables. You can even use one table per query and prepare the perfect table and partition for each query.

One of the primary reasons for denormalization is to optimize read performance. In relational databases, by using normalization, you often need to use JOIN operations to prepare a dataset. Since Cassandra doesn't support JOIN operations like traditional RDBMS systems, denormalization ensures that most queries are simple and direct fetch operations.

You can reduce latency by storing data in the exact structure or format that a client application requires.

Given Cassandra's distributed nature, attempting to mimic JOIN-like operations across multiple nodes would be highly inefficient and could result in significant latency. For that reason, JOINs are not possible in Cassandra. By denormalizing data, you ensure that all the data necessary to satisfy a particular query is collocated within the same partition so you can minimize cross-node communication.

Cassandra is optimized for write-heavy workloads. This means that even if denormalization results in storing redundant data across multiple tables, those writes are typically very efficient.

Denormalization, by eliminating the need for JOIN operations and ensuring data locality, allows the database to scale out more effectively. As you add more nodes to a Cassandra cluster, the system can continue to distribute data and load without the complexity of managing referential integrity or cross-node joins.

By focusing on query patterns and denormalizing data to suit specific queries, developers have a lot of flexibility in optimizing data access for various use cases.

It's important to remember that denormalization has drawbacks as well. You need more disk space if you store redundant data. However, it's worth noting that denormalization also has its downsides. Storing redundant data means you're using more disk space. Though storage costs have been decreasing, it's still a factor to consider. Redundant data can make updates more complex. You must ensure consistency across all places where the data exists, which can introduce challenges in ensuring data integrity. Over time, as application requirements change, a denormalized schema can become more challenging to evolve and refactor compared to a normalized schema.

Bucketing

Data bucketing can help prevent cluster load imbalance, which occurs when some Cassandra cluster nodes handle higher volumes of traffic or data than others, causing performance problems. Rather than creating a partition for every device, you could group data by time frames, such as weeks or months, to distribute the data and its I/O load more evenly.

A partition's row size should ideally be around 10MB and not exceed 100MB. Bucketing helps achieve this. If you don't have a *time* frame for *bucketing*, using a fabricated bucket_id can help this process, enabling the application to fetch data using these specific bucket IDs.

temperature_data			
device_id	pk,PK	uuid	*
date	pk,PK	dt	*
bucket	pk,PK	ts	*
reading_time	pk,CK, ↓	ts	*
temperature		double	
humidity		double	
location		text	

Figure 68 contains an example for this fabricated bucket_id:

temperature_data			
:: device_id	pk,PK	uuid	*
:: date	pk,PK	dt	*
:: bucket	pk,PK	ts	*
:: reading_time	pk,CK, ↓	ts	*
:: temperature		double	
:: humidity		double	
:: location		text	

Figure 68: Fabricated bucket_id.

```
CREATE TABLE iot.temperature_data (
    device_id UUID,
    date date,
    bucket int,
    reading_time timestamp,
    temperature double,
    humidity double,
    location text,
    PRIMARY KEY ((device_id,date,bucket)
reading_time)
) WITH CLUSTERING ORDER BY (reading_time DESC);

INSERT INTO iot.temperature_data (device_id,
date, bucket, reading_time, temperature,
humidity, location)
VALUES (uuid(), '2023-10-22', 1, '2023-10-22
12:01:00', 22.5, 60.0, 'Living Room');

INSERT INTO iot.temperature_data (device_id,
date, bucket, reading_time, temperature,
humidity, location)
VALUES (uuid(), '2023-10-22', 1, '2023-10-22
12:02:00', 22.6, 59.5, 'Living Room');

INSERT INTO iot.temperature_data (device_id,
date, bucket, reading_time, temperature,
humidity, location)
VALUES (uuid(), '2023-10-22', 2, '2023-10-22
12:31:00', 23.0, 58.5, 'Kitchen');
```

```
INSERT INTO iot.temperature_data (device_id,
date, bucket, reading_time, temperature,
humidity, location)
VALUES (uuid(), '2023-10-22', 2, '2023-10-22
12:32:00', 23.1, 58.0, 'Kitchen');
```

It helps for the distribution of the partition and takes the pressure of writing into a single node, but we would need to do reads through all buckets to get all the data per day with this table structure.

Partition size

The first thing to consider is the possible size of your table partitions. That is, are they too large? We define partitions in Cassandra by the total number of cells (values) they contain. Even though 2 billion cells per partition is the maximum for Cassandra, performance problems usually appear much earlier than that.

Using the following formula, you can get a good idea of the partition size:

$$N_v = N_r(N_c - N_{pk} - N_s) + N_s$$

The total count of values in a partition (Nv) equals the sum of the static columns (Ns) and the multiplication of the row count (Nr) with the values in each row. We calculate the values per row by subtracting the number of primary key columns (Npk) and static columns (Ns) from the total column count (Nc).

Tables can have their number of columns changed during runtime, but generally, it stays fixed. As a result, a partition's row count primarily determines its size. This is important when determining whether a partition may grow too big. Two billion values might seem a lot but they add up quickly in a sensor system that records tens or even hundreds of measurements per millisecond.

Let's look at **temperature_data** to analyze the partition size. The table has a total of six columns (Nc = 6), including three primary key columns (Npk = 3) and no static columns (Ns = 0). By applying these values to our formula, we get the result in Figure 69.

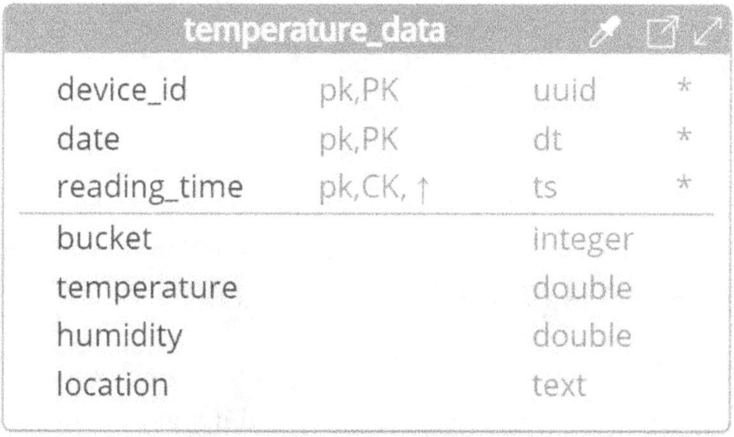

temperature_data			
device_id	pk,PK	uuid	*
date	pk,PK	dt	*
reading_time	pk,CK, ↑	ts	*
bucket		integer	
temperature		double	
humidity		double	
location		text	

Figure 69: Calculating partition size.

```
CREATE TABLE iot.temperature_data (
    device_id UUID,
    date date,
    reading_time timestamp,
```

```
    temperature double,
    humidity double,
    location text,
    PRIMARY KEY ((device_id,date) reading_time)
) WITH CLUSTERING ORDER BY (reading_time DESC);
```

$$Nv = Nr\,(\,6 - 3 - 0\,) + 0 = 3Nr$$

Accordingly, the total number of values in this table is three times the total number of rows. We still have to determine how many rows there will be, though. One way to achieve this is to think about the application's design. Each device's data and reading time are tracked in the table. We can calculate number of rows per partition by assuming that the system stores one row every second.

1 day: 86400 rows > Nr = 86400 rows

Nv = 259200 cells

This relatively small number of rows per partition is not going to get you in too much trouble, but if you start storing more data, or don't manage the size of the data well using TTL, you could start having issues. You still might want to look at breaking up this large partition, which we have seen in the bucketing part.

It is unlikely that this relatively low row count per partition will create issues, but it could if you start storing more data or don't use TTL to manage data size effectively. As covered in the bucketing section, it is also advisable to think about dividing this large partition.

Using average or nominal values, such as the number of rows, is simple as a basis for estimative sizing. Plan for the worst-case situation since these predictions usually come true even in well-designed systems.

Calculating partition size

Partition values aren't the only thing to consider when planning a cluster; it's also a good idea to calculate roughly how much space each table will require on disk. To determine the size (St) of a partition, use the following formula:

$$S_t = \sum_i sizeOf(c_{k_i}) + \sum_j sizeOf(c_{s_j}) + N_r \times \left(\sum_k sizeOf(c_{r_k}) + \sum_l sizeOf(c_{c_l}) \right) + N_v \times sizeOf(t_{avg})$$

Although this formula is a little more complicated than the last one, let's take it one step at a time. First, let's examine the notation. In this formula, 'ck' denotes the partition key columns, 'cs' for static columns, 'cr' for regular columns, and 'cc' for clustering columns.

The term "tavg" refers to the average amount of metadata, like timestamps, stored in each cell. This amount is usually estimated to be 8 bytes. You are familiar with the number of rows (Nr) and values (Nv) from previous calculations.

For every referenced column, the 'sizeOf()' function returns the byte size of the CQL data type.

It is necessary to sum up the partition key column sizes in the first part of the formula. We have **device_id** and **date** as partition keys for the **iot.temperature** data table in our example. With a 16-byte UUID for **device_id** and a 4-byte **date**, the partition key columns have a total size of 20 bytes.

The third term is more complex as it calculates the size of the cells in the partition. You need to add the sizes of the clustering and regular columns. The clustering column, which is the timestamp, is 8 bytes.

The location is roughly 15 bytes, and the double types (temperature and humidity), each of which is eight bytes, make up the three regular columns. The sum of the sizes of the clustering column (8 bytes) and the regular columns (31 bytes) equals 39 bytes. Multiply this value by the total number of rows (86,400) to finish this term, which equals 3,369,600 bytes, or 3.2 MB.

Cassandra stores metadata for every cell. The fourth term is just a total number of this metadata. The amount of metadata for a given cell varies depending on the type of data we store. Using the same formula, multiply the number of values (259200) in this table by 8 to get 1.98 MB.

You can get a final estimate by adding these terms together:

Partitionsize = 20 bytes+ 0 bytes + 3.2 MB+1.98 MB

The partition size on disk can be roughly calculated using this formula, which seems quite accurate and helpful. Considering that the partition must fit into a single node, the table design shouldn't put too much stress on disk storage.

Keep in mind that this estimate only takes into account one data replica. To calculate the total required capacity for each table, multiply the value obtained here by the number of partitions and replicas specified by the keyspace's replication strategy. This calculation will be useful when planning your cluster.[13]

Time to Live (TTL)

Time to Live (TTL) is a feature in Cassandra that allows for automatically deleting rows after a certain amount of time. TTL is an integer value representing the number of seconds a piece of data should live in the database from when it was inserted or updated.

When inserting or updating a row, you can specify a TTL value. Once that duration expires, Cassandra will mark the

---

[13] https://cassandra.apache.org/doc/stable/cassandra/data_modeling/data_modeling_refining.html.

associated data as "tombstones". Cassandra will delete this data in subsequent compactions.

Cassandra does not immediately remove this data after the TTL has expired. Instead, it is marked for deletion and removed during the next compaction cycle. Until compaction occurs, the data will be invisible to reads.

Here are a few TTL use cases:

- **Session data:** For applications where session data is stored, and the data becomes irrelevant after the session expires.

- **Caching:** Where the data is only valid for a certain duration.

- **Time-series data:** When only recent data is of interest and older data can be safely discarded.

TTLs can help save storage space, especially in use cases where data becomes obsolete after a certain period of time.

Expired TTLs can influence read performance. When we read data with an expired TTL, Cassandra will recognize that the data has expired and will not return it, but reading a lot of expired data that has not yet been compacted can slow down queries.

When data expires due to TTL, it creates a tombstone (a deletion marker). Tombstones are necessary to handle distributed deletes in Cassandra but can affect read and write performance if they accumulate. Properly tuning compaction strategies and understanding the impact of tombstones are important when using TTLs. If you have time-series data or data with a set TTL in Cassandra, using the Time Window Compaction Strategy can help optimize storage and improve query performance by handling old, expired data efficiently.

Composite keys

Composite keys in Cassandra's data modeling provide a combination of partition and clustering columns, enabling fine-grained data organization and efficient querying. Developers can use composite keys to ensure data distribution across nodes while maintaining a sorted order within partitions. This dual benefit facilitates rapid data retrieval for specific ranges or slices of data, such as retrieving a particular user's activity for a specified date range. Moreover, composite keys support scalability by evenly distributing data load and provide flexibility in modeling complex access patterns, allowing developers to optimize for both write and read operations in large-scale, distributed environments.

Compaction

Compaction is a crucial part of Apache Cassandra performance tuning that you should know about.

Cassandra optimizes disk space and cleans up old data through the process of compression. The performance of your system, disk I/O, and the speed of read/write operations are all affected by the compaction strategy you choose. Let's look at the various Cassandra compaction strategies:

- **Size-Tiered Compaction Strategy (STCS):** Best for write-heavy workloads and large deletes. When STCS collects enough similar-sized SSTables, it initiates compaction. It then combines them into a single larger SSTable. It is good for efficient disk I/O and faster write operations but not ideal for read-heavy workloads, and markers for deleted data (tombstones) could persist for quite some time.

- **Leveled Compaction Strategy (LCS):** Best for read-heavy workloads and applications requiring low-latency data retrieval. It divides SSTables into levels and runs compaction to ensure that we optimize each level for read operations. LCS has better read performance and faster deletion of tombstones. On the other hand, it includes more disk I/O and it can be slower on writes.

- **Time Window Compaction Strategy (TWCS):** Best for time-series data like IoT sensor data or logs. It compacts SSTables based on the time window of the data they hold, making it efficient for TTL (time-to-live) expirations. The ability to handle TTL-based deletions effectively and optimize for time-series query patterns are advantages. One drawback is that, if not configured properly, it could result in multiple small SSTables.

- **Date Tiered Compaction Strategy (DTCS) [Deprecated]:** Best for time-series data but is now deprecated in favor of TWCS. It is similar to TWCS but is less efficient in managing TTL-based deletions. It's recommended to use TWCS over DTCS for new implementations. If you have write-heavy workloads with minimal reads, STCS could be your best choice. LCS provides an advantage with its optimized read paths for read-heavy or balanced workloads. If you're dealing with time-series data, TWCS is typically the preferred strategy, especially if TTL is required.

If you have write-heavy workloads with minimal reads, STCS could be your best choice. LCS provides an advantage with its optimized read paths for read-heavy or balanced workloads. If you're dealing with time-series data, TWCS is typically the preferred strategy, especially if TTL is required.

Choose the correct compaction strategy for optimal performance in your Cassandra database. Test each strategy in a staging environment representative of your production workload for the best results.

Batch operations

Cassandra is designed with a write-heavy pattern in mind, prioritizing fast and efficient write operations. Cassandra appends writes to a commit log for durability before being written to an in-memory structure known as memtable. Data is flushed from the memtable to an immutable SSTable on disk once it is full. Writes are extremely efficient because they only append data, preventing costly disk searches.

Also, Cassandra's distributed design makes it easy to spread write workloads across multiple nodes, simplifying high-volume write operations. Because of this feature, Cassandra is ideal for applications with a large volume of writes, such as event logging, monitoring systems, and time-series data.

With Cassandra's *batch* feature, you can combine several DML operations (such as INSERT, UPDATE, and DELETE) into one atomic action, guaranteeing that no operation will fail unless each of them succeeds. While they ensure atomicity, batches are not primarily designed for performance enhancement. In fact, misuse can lead to decreased performance.

We can log batches in CQL (the default, providing stronger atomicity via a batch log) or unlogged (faster, but with fewer atomicity guarantees). It's critical to use batches wisely, ideally containing data from a single partition, to reduce coordination overhead and prevent excessively big batches that could overburden the system.

Ideally, using a single partition, you can insert multiple rows:

```
BEGIN BATCH
  INSERT INTO users (user_id, username, email)
VALUES (1, 'John', 'john@email.com');
  INSERT INTO users (user_id, username, email)
VALUES (2, 'Sara', 'sara@email.com');
APPLY BATCH;

You can also mix different operations;

BEGIN BATCH
  INSERT INTO users (user_id, username, email)
VALUES (3, 'Mike', 'mike@email.com');
  UPDATE users SET email = 'newjohn@email.com'
WHERE user_id = 1;
  DELETE FROM users WHERE user_id = 2;
APPLY BATCH;

You can also set a specific timestamp for all
operations in batch:

BEGIN BATCH USING TIMESTAMP 123456789
  INSERT INTO users (user_id, username, email)
VALUES (4, 'Emma', 'emma@email.com');
  DELETE FROM users WHERE user_id = 3;
APPLY BATCH;
```

Cassandra log batches by default if multiple partitions are involved, but you can change it to unlogged batches. It uses batch with logging enabled when automaticity is needed. Using the batch log incurs a performance penalty because it needs to write to the other nodes. Single-partition batch operations are unlogged by default.[14]

Counters

In Cassandra, counters are a specialized column type designed to hold distributed incremental values. Counters support atomic increments and decrements, making them ideal for use cases like tracking page views, likes, or any scenario where a value needs to be incremented or decremented in a distributed and concurrent environment.

Internally, each node tracks its local changes to a counter, ensuring high write availability and scalability. There are a few things to remember. First, you can't use counters alongside regular columns in the same table. Second, you can't set specific values with them, only incremental updates. We must understand their distributed nature and limitations to make effective use of them.

```
CREATE TABLE page_views ( page_id UUID PRIMARY
KEY, view_count COUNTER
);
UPDATE page_views SET view_count = view_count + 1
WHERE page_id = 9d323eb4-c66a-479c-a701-
5366d7fe46c1;
```

---

[14] https://docs.datastax.com/en/cql-oss/3.x/cql/cql_reference/cqlBatch.html#:~:text=If%20multiple%20partit ions%20are%20involved,serialized%20batch%20as%20blob%20data.

```
UPDATE page_views SET view_count = view_count - 1
WHERE page_id = 9d323eb4-c66a-479c-a701-
5366d7fe46c1;
```

Cassandra data modeling anti-patterns

Lightweight Transactions (LWT)

Lightweight Transactions (LWT) in Cassandra provide a mechanism to ensure atomicity and isolation, principles commonly associated with traditional relational databases. LWTs enable condition-based operations, such as "insert a value only if it doesn't already exist."

The Paxos consensus protocol is used under the hood to achieve this consistency across the distributed nodes. The consensus protocol Paxos, created by Leslie Lamport is a distributed systems technique that enables different nodes to agree on a single value even in the event of a failure It is tailored for reliability and efficiency in scenarios, even during failures. In Paxos, nodes suggest values, and through sequential voting rounds, they collectively determine one value for acceptance. While powerful in ensuring data integrity in concurrent environments, LWTs have a performance cost due to the additional coordination required among nodes.

We should only use LWTs occasionally and where the possible performance trade-offs justify the strong consistency requirements. Let's say you have a **users** table and want to insert a new user only if that user does not already exist. You can use IF NOT EXISTS to achieve this:

```
INSERT INTO users (user_id, username, email)
VALUES (1, 'John', 'john@email.com') IF NOT
EXISTS;
```

You can conditionally delete rows as well. The following query deletes a user only if the email matches a specific value:

```
DELETE FROM users WHERE user_id = 1 IF email =
'john@email.com';
```

Accord is a proposed mechanism to improve the performance of conditional updates in Apache Cassandra. It offers an alternative to the traditional lightweight transactions, which use the Paxos consensus protocol and come with certain performance overheads. Accord's primary goal is to provide similar consistency guarantees as LWTs but with reduced latency and fewer round trips between nodes, enhancing the efficiency of conditional operations.

Tombstones

Tombstones are markers in Cassandra that indicate the deletion of data. While they are necessary for a distributed system to propagate deletions, too many tombstones can cause performance issues. Accumulating a large number of tombstones has an impact on read performance because Cassandra must scan over these markers, resulting in increased read latency. Furthermore, reconciling and removing tombstones during compaction can be resource-intensive, resulting in increased I/O and CPU usage. Tombstones can also take up unnecessary space if not cleaned up regularly through compaction.

As a result, in Cassandra data modeling, it's critical to create schemas and access patterns that minimize tombstone creation to ensure optimal system performance and resource utilization.

To avoid tombstones in Cassandra data modeling, you can use "compaction-friendly" data models, such as time-window-based partitioning for time-series data, where we can drop entire old partitions rather than deleting individual records. Leveraging these techniques and understanding when and how often deletions occur, can significantly minimize the creation of tombstones and their associated overhead.

Materialized views and secondary indexes

In Cassandra, options like materialized views and secondary indexes provide more ways to query data. However, they also bring considerable downsides that may conflict with the principles of efficient data modeling.

Materialized views are automatically updated tables reflecting the primary table's data, but they can lead to write amplification, putting extra load on write operations.

Secondary indexes enable querying on non-primary key columns but can lead to uneven data distribution across nodes, resulting in imbalanced partitions or "hotspots" and potentially inefficient reads. Both these features also increase the burden of maintenance activities, such as compaction. While they improve querying capabilities, the drawbacks often outweigh their benefits, particularly in environments with heavy write operations or large-scale data. This situation encourages exploring alternative data modeling strategies like denormalization or using Storage Attached Indexes in Cassandra to achieve better performance.

Unfrozen collection types

The term "unfrozen" typically refers to collections (such as lists, sets, or maps) stored in their modifiable state. Unfrozen data types introduce complexity and potential pitfalls into Cassandra data modeling while providing flexibility for in-place updates.

First, updates to individual elements within an unfrozen collection generate tombstones (markers for deletions), which can accumulate and affect read performance. These tombstones also add overhead during the compaction process. If the unfrozen collection grows significantly, it can result in oversized partitions, leading to read and write inefficiencies. Lastly, using modifiable collections without proper forethought can also cause unexpected versioning issues in a distributed environment. So, even though unfrozen collections are versatile, they are frequently not the best option for Cassandra data modeling because of possible performance and maintenance issues.

Query-level antipatterns

Query-level anti-patterns in CQL (Cassandra Query Language) for Apache Cassandra are inefficient practices that can lead to poor performance, scalability issues, and other challenges. Here are some common query-level anti-patterns in CQL:

- **Using Allow Filtering:** Using ALLOW FILTERING in queries can lead to performance issues. This command forces Cassandra to scan through more data than necessary, which is inefficient, especially for large datasets. It's generally better to structure your data model to avoid needing ALLOW FILTERING.

- **Using IN inefficiently:** The IN clause in CQL is typically used to query multiple partition keys. Cassandra is designed to be efficient when reading from a single partition, but when you use IN to query multiple partitions, it can result in a scattered read operation across different nodes in the cluster. This kind of operation is less efficient and can put a significant load on the cluster, especially if the partitions are large or the number of partitions in the IN list is high.

- **Using aggregations:** Aggregation operations, like sum, average, or count, require data to be collected and processed across multiple nodes. This is inherently inefficient in a distributed system where data is spread across different nodes in a cluster. You can update the aggregates on-the-fly or implement aggregation on the client side. Another solution could be using Apache Spark.

Additional Cassandra features

Cassandra index types

Using a secondary index, you can query a table with a column that isn't typically queryable. Unlike the primary index linked to the primary key column, we can create a secondary index on non-primary key columns for efficient data retrieval based on those columns.

However, there are some drawbacks to using secondary indexes in Cassandra, such as potentially increasing disk space usage and increasing write operations, which can affect performance. Secondary index queries, which result in distributed scans, can be slow, especially when dealing with columns that don't have many unique values.

Distributed systems add complexity and efficiency issues when we handle these indexes across nodes.

Additionally, secondary indexes do not immediately reflect changes because they are only *eventually consistent*. You must be careful when using secondary indexes because not all query types are supported. It is important to thoroughly evaluate the application's unique needs and performance tests before deciding to use secondary indexes since other methods, like Storage Attached Indexes (SAIs) or denormalized tables, may provide better performance and manageability. SAIs are compatible with DataStax Astra DB and DataStax Enterprise (DSE) database and will be available in Cassandra with CEP-7.[15] Its advantages over more conventional indexing methods in Cassandra are unique and include:

- Enabling vector search suitable for AI-based applications
- Common data sharing across multiple indexes within the same table
- Efficient write-time scalability
- Substantial reduction in disk usage
- Excellent performance on numeric range queries
- Zero-copy streaming for index data.

---

[15] https://cwiki.apache.org/confluence/display/CASSANDRA/CEP-7%3A+Storage+Attached+Index.

Basically, SAI improves Cassandra's indexing capabilities by allowing column-level indexes for almost all CQL data types. Multiple types of filters, such as vector embeddings, logical operators (AND, OR), numeric ranges, text equality, and tokenized data, can be used to execute queries with SAI.[16]

SAI improves development efficiency by speeding up the process of developing applications by improving the performance of queries on indexed columns. It indexes both in-memory memtables and on-disk SSTables with seamless integration with the Cassandra storage engine. Additionally, SAI is compatible with zero-copy streaming, meaning that we stream the indexes and SSTables simultaneously when nodes in a cluster are bootstrapped or decommissioned, removing the need for serialization or rebuilding at the receiving end.

Compared to other indexing techniques currently available in Cassandra, SAI performs better. It uses less disk space and provides more functionality than a conventional secondary index(2i). As a result, the total cost of operating and disk infrastructure goes down. When it comes to critical performance metrics like write and read speeds, SAI outperforms other options in terms of latency and

---

[16] https://docs.datastax.com/en/cql/astra/docs/developing/indexing/sai/sai-concepts.html.

throughput, making it the most effective and productive indexing solution for Cassandra.

With Hackolade Studio, it is easy to generate the syntactically correct CQL script for the creation of indexes, simply by filling out the corresponding form dynamically presenting the different options.

Consistency levels

Consistency levels control how many replicas must acknowledge a read or write operation before it is considered successful. This is critical for balancing data availability and accuracy in a distributed database system. Here are some common consistency levels:

- **ONE:** Only one replica must acknowledge the read or write operation. This is the lowest level of consistency and offers the highest availability but the least consistency.

- **QUORUM:** Most replicas for a given piece of data must respond. This provides a good balance of availability and consistency.

- **LOCAL_QUORUM:** Similar to QUORUM, but only considers replicas in the local datacenter. Useful for reducing latency in multi-datacenter configurations.

- **EACH_QUORUM:** Each datacenter must have a quorum of nodes acknowledge the operation.

- **ALL:** All replicas must acknowledge the operation. This provides the highest consistency but the lowest availability.

- **LOCAL_ONE:** Only one replica in the local datacenter must acknowledge the operation.

Consistency levels impact data modeling in a number of ways:

- **Data integrity:** You can affect the reliability of your data by choosing a consistency level. While a lower consistency level may result in reduced latency and improved availability, it also increases the chances that you will read inconsistent or stale data.

- **Read and write patterns:** Your application's read/write patterns can help you choose the right consistency level. A write-heavy application, for example, might benefit from a lower read consistency setting with a higher write consistency setting to guarantee data integrity.

- **Multi-datacenter configurations:** In Apache Cassandra multi-datacenter configurations, the consistency level is critical for balancing performance with data availability. When a consistency level like QUORUM or LOCAL QUORUM is selected, Cassandra ensures that most replicas in the local or global cluster respond before considering a read or write operation successful. This improves data consistency but may result in increased latency, especially if datacenter coordination is required to achieve the required consistency level. Using a lower consistency level, such as ONE or LOCAL ONE, allows for faster operations by requiring only a response from one replica — either in any datacenter or the local datacenter. However, it may risk data consistency because it does not ensure that the most recent write is read.

- **Use-case specific:** Some use cases may naturally require higher consistency levels. For example, strong consistency guarantees may be necessary for financial applications to meet compliance standards.

When working with Cassandra data modeling, knowing the consequences of tunable consistency is important. You can tailor it to meet the application's unique requirements while maintaining consistency, availability, and performance.

Vector search and LLMs

Vector databases are becoming essential in today's data-centric world, particularly for tasks requiring complex, multi-dimensional data analysis. This includes recommendation systems, searching for similar items, and powering chatbots. Unlike traditional databases, built for structured data and exact matches, vector databases are designed to handle and quickly search through data in vector form. This makes them ideal for recognizing patterns and similarities in high-dimensional data spaces.

These databases use distance metrics to measure how close vectors are to each other, and they work great with scenarios where understanding relationships between data points is more important than finding an exact match. This is particularly useful in fields like image and voice recognition, recommending products or content, and semantic searches. As the amount of complex data continues to grow and the need to make sense of this data becomes more crucial, vector databases are emerging as an important tool for managing and extracting valuable insights from it.

A vector is a mathematical entity represented by a sequence of numbers or coordinates. These coordinates locate the vector within a multi-dimensional space.

Embeddings, a specialized form of vectors, are extensively utilized in machine learning and natural language processing. They transform complex, high-dimensional data, such as text or images, into vectors of lower dimensions. An example is word embeddings, which map words to vectors, positioning words with similar meanings closer together in the vector space.

Vector databases are uniquely tailored to store and retrieve vectors and, in the list below, you can see how vector databases differ from traditional databases:

- **Vector Storage:** These databases hold vectors or embeddings, typically outputs from machine learning models. They convert complex data types such as text, images, or audio into a numerical vector format.

- **Efficient Indexing:** Vector databases use specialized indexing methods to retrieve data quickly. Rather than the more traditional sorting-based indexing, they use algorithms like approximate nearest neighbor (ANN). Using metrics such as cosine similarity or Euclidean distance, these algorithms quickly find the vectors that are nearest to a query vector.

- **Vector-Based Querying:** The input query is converted to a vector as part of the querying procedure. After choosing a distance metric, the database will locate and return vectors relative to your query vector. Recommendation engines, image/voice recognition systems, and searches based on semantic text understanding all benefit greatly from this feature.

OSS Cassandra will support Vector Search with CEP-30. The aim is to implement approximate nearest neighbor (ANN) vector search capability in Apache Cassandra using storage-attached indexes (SAI). Datastax's managed solution Astra and DSE already has this available, as well as text search capabilities.

Chebotko's Diagram

An effective data model may be challenging to design due to Cassandra's unique architecture. This is where Chebotko's Diagram becomes important. Artem Chebotko's diagrammatic approach helps to simplify the Cassandra data model creation process.

Chebotko's Diagram is a data model visualization technique tailored to Apache Cassandra. It clearly represents tables, columns, and relationships in the Cassandra database. The diagram has several components:

- **Tables:** The main components are tables (represented by rectangles). Each table contains a partition key, clustering columns, and other columns showing how data is organized and accessed.

- **Partition Keys**: The partition keys in the tables determine the distribution of data among the nodes in the Cassandra cluster.

- **Clustering Columns**: These columns define the order of data within a partition and are important for query efficiency.

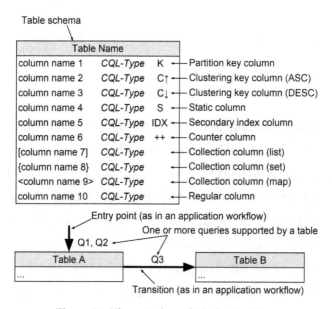

Figure 70: The notation of Chebotko Diagrams.

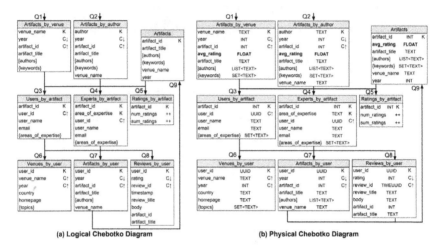

(a) Logical Chebotko Diagram   (b) Physical Chebotko Diagram

Figure 71: Chebotko Diagram example.

Think about making a data model to store information from sensors. The main query could be retrieving sensor data for a particular device over a given time period. The Chebotko Diagram in this situation will include a table called **sensor_data** with columns for **device_id** (the partition key), reading_time (the clustering column), and other data points like **temperature**, **humidity**, and so on. Figure 72 shows that the partition key is **device_id**, ensuring that data for the same device is stored on the same node.

Figure 72: Entity supporting querying data over time.

We can use the **reading_time** column to efficiently query data over a time range.[17]

Stargate APIs

Stargate is an open-source data gateway that provides API, data, and schema operations for databases. When used with Apache Cassandra, it provides a variety of APIs for interacting with the database that wouldn't need the usage of the native Cassandra Query Language (CQL).

Here's a brief overview of Stargate APIs for Cassandra:[18]

- **REST:** This API enables developers to execute CRUD activities on Cassandra using normal HTTP techniques. It abstracts away the CQL and gives a more familiar interface for developers familiar with RESTful services.

- **GraphQL:** Stargate offers a GraphQL API for schema and CRUD operations. Developers can use the API to create, modify, and delete keyspaces and tables. It offers flexible querying of Cassandra using GraphQL queries for data operations.

---

[17] https://www.researchgate.net/publication/308856170_A_Big_Data_Modeling_Methodology_for_Apache_Cassandra.

[18] https://stargate.io/docs/latest/develop/dev-with-doc.html.

- **DocumentAPI:** This API helps you to use JSON documents or models without worrying about a predefined schema. As the Document API uses schemaless data, no data modeling is required! It generates the necessary structure on the fly, allowing you to use any JSON layout. It also has powerful search capabilities, allowing you to look for specific information within a single document or across a collection. You can retrieve the entire JSON document or just a portion from any collection. This API is compatible with storage-attached indexes, allowing for more query options and making development easier and faster. If you're working with structured or semi-structured data, the API also supports JSON schemas, which improves testing, data checking, and API documentation.

- **gRPC:** gRPC is a modern, open-source remote procedure call (RPC) framework. It enables transparent communication between client and server applications and makes it easier to build connected systems. The Stargate gRPC API creates language-specific queries in CQL to use with any Cassandra deployment.

Spark Cassandra Connector

Several factors make the Spark-Cassandra Connector a valuable tool. As an example, it enables the integration of a general-purpose cluster-computing framework, Apache Spark, with the scalable and highly available NoSQL database, Apache Cassandra. The merging of the two systems' scalability and efficiency makes complicated analytics and data transformations much easier and faster to accomplish.

Including the Spark-Cassandra Connector library in your Spark project is the first step in using the connector. After that, you can use Spark's API to read data from Cassandra tables into DataFrames or Resilient Distributed Datasets (RDDs). Then, you can manipulate the data as needed. The fact that we can execute all of these tasks using plain old Spark code makes it easy to build robust data pipelines that take advantage of the best features of both systems. Reduced data transfer times and network burden are two additional benefits of the connector's improved data localization, which tries to process data on the Cassandra node where it is stored.[19]

---

[19] https://github.com/datastax/spark-cassandra-connector.

Data migration methods

Zero Down Migrator (ZDM)

ZDM for Cassandra is a useful tool for ensuring successful and downtime-free data migration between Cassandra clusters. This will keep your application running smoothly throughout migration, preventing service interruptions. The Zero Down Migrator uses a lightweight proxy such as ZDM Proxy to handle real-time data synchronization between source and destination clusters. The Zero Downtime Migrator Proxy (ZDM Proxy), part of the Zero Down Migrator for Cassandra, manages communication between your application and the Cassandra clusters while you migrate. It is in charge of synchronizing and routing data so that it can be transferred seamlessly between the source and destination clusters. It is the proxy's responsibility to correctly redirect read and write requests. For anyone interested, ZDM Proxy is freely available in its public GitHub repository as open-source software (OSS), https://github.com/datastax/zdm-proxy.

With ZDM's additional rollback options, you can migrate without any worries. Businesses that rely on data services and cannot afford any downtime during transfers will find this technology particularly useful.

Figure 73: Zero Down Migrator (ZDM)[20]

DSBulk

The DataStax Bulk Loader, or DSBulk, is a command-line tool for efficiently importing, exporting, and counting data in Apache Cassandra databases. It is fast and flexible, making it ideal for bulk migration for the applications. DSBulk can help with data migration, Cassandra loading, and data exporting.

You can specify the output target directory to unload data.

```
dsbulk unload -k keyspace_name -t table_name -
url /path/to/output/directory/
```

DSBulk then fetches the data from the keyspace and table in Cassandra.

---

[20] https://docs.datastax.com/en/astra-serverless/docs/migrate/rollback.html.

Ensure your data is in a compatible format, such as CSV or JSON, before loading it into a Cassandra table. You can then use the command line to run a DSBulk command, specifying details such as the keyspace, table, and location of your data file, among other parameters.

For example, the command could be:

```
dsbulk load -k keyspace_name -t table_name -url
/path/to/datafile.csv.
```

DSBulk handles mapping data fields to Cassandra columns, which you can customize with the -m flag if needed. The tool also splits the data into manageable batches, which are then written concurrently to the Cassandra cluster for optimal performance. DSBulk provides real-time information such as throughput and total number of records handled throughout this procedure.

Although DSBulk works well with smaller data sets, CDM is generally more efficient for migrating large volumes of data. CDM also eliminates the need to handle files.

Cassandra Data Migrator

Cassandra Data Migrator is a tool for migrating keyspaces and tables within the same Apache Cassandra cluster or between clusters. It's especially useful for schema migrations, upgrades, and moving to a newly configured cluster. Using a data migrator can ensure a more efficient, consistent, and safe data transfer process, saving time and lowering the risk of errors. Whether upgrading to a new version of Cassandra, changing your data model, or scaling up, Cassandra data migrator makes the data migration process much easier and less error-prone. For example:

Data Migration:

```
./spark-submit --properties-file cdm.properties -
-conf
spark.cdm.schema.origin.keyspaceTable="<keyspacen
ame>.<tablename>" --master "local[*]" --driver-
memory 25G --executor-memory 25G --class
com.datastax.cdm.job.Migrate cassandra-data-
migrator-4.x.x.jar &> logfile_name_$(date
+%Y%m%d_%H_%M).txt
```

Data Validation:

```
./spark-submit --properties-file cdm.properties -
-conf
spark.cdm.schema.origin.keyspaceTable="<keyspacen
ame>.<tablename>" --master "local[*]" --driver-
memory 25G --executor-memory 25G --class
com.datastax.cdm.job.DiffData cassandra-data-
migrator-4.x.x.jar &> logfile_name_$(date
+%Y%m%d_%H_%M).txt
```

SStable loader

You can find the *SSTableLoader* tool in Apache Cassandra. Its major purpose is to help efficiently load large data sets into a Cassandra cluster. To import Cassandra's immutable data files, known as SSTables, the

SSTableLoader is used instead of DSBulk or Cassandra Data Migrator. Its native integration with the storage engine greatly improves the efficiency of importing massive datasets.

You would first create SSTables that are compatible with the Cassandra version you are using. We can manage this using offline tools or by generating them on another Cassandra node. You should confirm that the schema definitions in the source and target are the same.

To generate raw Cassandra data files locally for bulk loading into your cluster, you can use the SSTableWriter API. To generate SSTable files from external data without getting into the details of internal of how those files map to the underlying storage engine, Cassandra's source code contains the CQLSSTableWriter implementation. Import the org.apache.cassandra.io.sstable.CQLSSTableWriter class, specify the data schema, a writer for the schema, and a prepared insert statement to import the data.[21]

After preparing the SSTables, we can import the data into the target cluster with the sstableloader command. The

---

[21] https://docs.datastax.com/en/cassandra-oss/3.x/cassandra/tools/toolsBulkloader.html#:~:text=Provides%20the%20ability%20to%20bulk,replication%20strategy%2C%20and%20restore%20snapshots.

tool will follow the partitioning design, and the data will be distributed correctly among all nodes.

```
sstableloader -d 192.168.1.1
/path/to/sstable_dir/keyspace_name/table_name-
UUID/
```

In this example:

'-d 192.168.1.1': Specifies one node in the cluster (Cassandra will find the rest).

'/path/to/sstable_dir/keyspace_name/table_name-UUID/': This is the path to the SSTables you wish to load.

COPY

One useful tool for working with Cassandra tables is the COPY command in CQL (Cassandra Query Language). Either loading data from CSV files into Cassandra in bulk or exporting table data to a CSV file for analysis or backup is simplified with this method. For example:

Exporting users table into a csv file:

```
COPY my_keyspace.users (id, name, email) TO
'path/to/users_export.csv';
```

Importing into users table from a csv file:

```
COPY my_keyspace.users (id, name, email) FROM
'path/to/users.csv';
```

Benchmarking tools

NoSqlBench

Test your NoSQL databases with NoSQLBench, an open-source tool that's both free and easy to use. It supports multiple database drivers and provides a flexible way to build workloads, which both ensure that the tests are realistic representations of the actual world.

NoSQLBench's customizable scripting and workload features allow you to test your database in a realistic environment, which sets it apart from the other options. In addition to raw statistics, you will receive additional information on the performance of your database, which will provide insights into its inner workings. Furthermore, it is constantly improving due to the community's regular updates and the fact that it is open-source.

```
./nb run start driver=cql workload=cql-keyvalue
tags=phase:main cycles=100k cyclerate=5000
threads=50 --progress console:2s
```

- **start** executes the workload statements asynchronously

- **workload=cql-keyvalue** identifies the workload file

- **tags=phase:main** identifies the section to run within the workload file

- **cycles=100k** tells nb to run the section 100,000 times

- **cyclerate=5000** limits the test to 5,000 operations per second

- **threads=50** the default is to use one thread. Setting this parameter allows NoSQLBench the necessary concurrency for a significant workload.

- **--progress console:2s** sets the progress reporting interval to two seconds

Cassandra-stress

We can use Cassandra-stress for simple load testing and benchmarking. It's critical for understanding how different data models perform under various types of stress. By simulating real-world conditions, this tool helps identify potential performance issues and bottlenecks in a controlled setting.[22] An example of a mixed-workload scenario using the Cassandra-stress tool:

```
cassandra-stress mixed ratio(write=1, read=3)
n=100000 cl=ONE -pop dist=UNIFORM(1..1000000) -
schema keyspace="keyspace1" -mode native cql3 -
rate threads\>=16 threads\<=256 -log
file=~/mixed_autorate_50r50w_1M.log
```

---

[22] https://docs.datastax.com/en/dse/5.1/docs/tooling/cassandra-stress-tool.html.

- The value of n in the read phase differs from that in the write phase. n records are written during the write phase. However, if n is too large, reading all the records for simple testing during the read phase is inconvenient. When validating a cluster's persistent storage systems, n does not need to be large. The -pop *dist=UNIFORM(1..1000000)* option instructs the program to select keys uniformly distributed between 1 and 1,000,000 from the n=100,000 operations.

- The rate section tells cassandra-stress to automatically attempt different numbers of client threads and not test less that 16 or more than 256 client threads.

```
threads>=N run at least this many clients
concurrently. Default is 4.
threads<=N run at most this many clients
concurrently. Default is 1000.
```

Use case examples

Internet of Things (IoT)

As discussed throughout the Cassandra use cases section, we can frequently use Cassandra for IOT use cases because it provides low-latency access, scalability, and high availability, in addition to the features needed for large-scale, high-throughput time-series data storage. It is an excellent option for Internet of Things applications due to its decentralized nature, flexibility, and capacity to manage deployments in different geographical locations.

temperature_data			
device_id	pk,PK	uuid	*
date	pk,PK	dt	*
reading_time	pk,CK, ↑	ts	*
bucket		integer	
temperature		double	
humidity		double	
location		text	

Figure 74: An initial table for storing temperature data.

```
CREATE TABLE iot.temperature_data (
    device_id UUID,
    date date,
    reading_time timestamp,
    temperature double,
    humidity double,
    location text,
    PRIMARY KEY ((device_id,date) reading_time)
) WITH CLUSTERING ORDER BY (reading_time DESC);
```

The Time to Live (TTL) parameter is essential for device and sensor data lifecycle control.

Internet of Things (IoT) systems can automatically delete unnecessary data using TTL, which saves space and money. This flexibility enables IoT applications to optimize data storage, comply with data privacy regulations, and maintain query performance while complying with data retention expectations. Additionally, a parameter known as "unsafe aggressive sstable expiration" is available: Mutations in different sstables might cause sstables to remain after the TTL period, and queries could read more sstables than required.

You can use "unsafe aggressive sstable expiration" to remove the sstables once the TTL period has passed. By selecting this option, Cassandra will discard entire SSTables when they expire, regardless of whether the partitions are present in other SSTables or not.[23]

As we saw in the align and refine steps, we need to gather the query requirements before starting the physical design. We need to verify the partition size per device and month if we need to query by month. We can select a partition per device and month if the disk size is less than 100 MB and ideally less than 10 MB. By storing the date and reading time in the clustering key, we can also use it to search for specific ranges of these values.

temperature_data_by_month			
device_id	pk,PK	uuid	*
year	pk,PK	integer	*
month	pk,PK	integer	*
date	pk,CK, ↓	dt	*
reading_time	pk,CK, ↓	ts	*
temperature		double	
humidity		double	
location		text	

Figure 75: Temperature data by month.

---

[23] https://cassandra.apache.org/doc/latest/cassandra/operating/compaction/twcs.html.

```
CREATE TABLE iot.temperature_data_by_month (
    device_id UUID,
    year int,
    month int,
    date date,
    reading_time timestamp,
    temperature double,
    humidity double,
    location text,
    PRIMARY KEY ((device_id,year,month),date,
reading_time)
) WITH CLUSTERING ORDER BY (date
desc,reading_time DESC);
```

If we have large amounts of data per device and month, we need to add bucketing to the table to make the partitions more manageable. Since we already have a date column in the table, we can add that to the partition after calculating if the partition size is ideally less than 10MB.

temperature_data_by_date			
device_id	pk,PK	uuid	*
year	pk,PK	integer	*
month	pk,PK	integer	*
date	pk,PK	dt	*
reading_time	pk,CK, ↓	ts	*
temperature		double	
humidity		double	
location		text	

Figure 76: With bucketing.

```
CREATE TABLE iot.temperature_data_by_date (
    device_id UUID,
    year int,
    month int,
    date date,
    reading_time timestamp,
    temperature double,
    humidity double,
    location text,
    PRIMARY KEY ((device_id,year,month,date),
reading_time)
```

```
) WITH CLUSTERING ORDER BY (date
desc,reading_time DESC);
```

There may be a requirement for monthly aggregated data for analytical queries or auditing when preparing the application table for IoT. In this case, you can aggregate the metrics per month instead of date and store in a monthly table as well.

We can use separate TTLs should for the monthly and original date-partitioned tables. A streaming solution or application can achieve this aggregation before writing multiple different tables:

```
CREATE TABLE iot.temperature_data_by_month (
    device_id UUID,
    year int,
    month int,
    date date,
    temperature_avg double,
    humidity_avg double,
    location text,
    PRIMARY KEY ((device_id,year,month),date,
reading_time)
) WITH CLUSTERING ORDER BY (date
desc,reading_time DESC);
```

Alternatively, you can use the Spark Cassandra Connector to add a new layer to Cassandra. This way, you can run a variety of auditing and analytical queries without worrying about partition keys or primary key restrictions. Another option is to send data changes to a different database that's better suited for analytics or store them in S3 using Change Data Capture (CDC). CDC is an alternative for sending data changes to a different database better suited for analytics or storing them in S3 or another relational database using Change Data Capture.

Retail

Vector databases and Large Language Models (LLMs) such as OpenAI's GPT series have the potential to have a significant impact on the retail industry in different ways:

- **Product Recommendations:** Based on their properties, we can represent products as high-dimensional vectors in vector databases. Retailers can deliver more accurate product recommendations to consumers by comparing the similarity of vectors.

- **Visual Search:** Customers can upload an image of a product they're interested in, and the vector database can compare image vectors and find products with similar visual features.

- **Customer Segmentation:** Retailers can group similar customers together for targeted marketing campaigns by representing customer data as vectors.

- **Sentiment Analysis:** Vector databases can help analyze customer reviews, comments, and feedback to gain insights into customer sentiments about products or the overall brand.

In this use case, we will explore the process of effectively preparing and implementing a solution for identifying and retrieving similar products based on image analysis. To begin with, we must create the table that will contain the embeddings along with the product's color, name, and category. We selected creating the partitions with item_category so we'll check the similarities between the same categories.

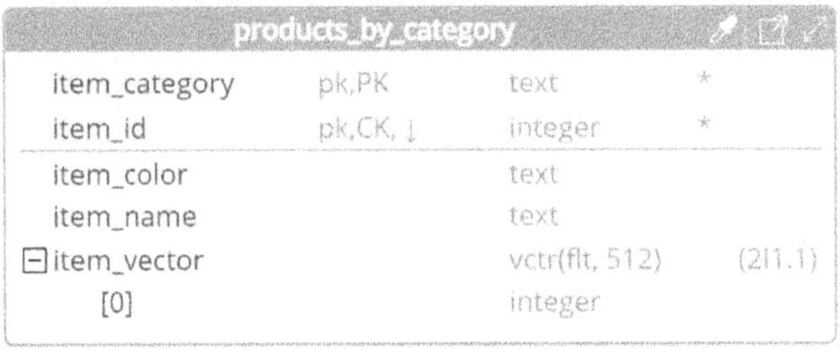

products_by_category			
item_category	pk,PK	text	*
item_id	pk,CK, ↓	integer	*
item_color		text	
item_name		text	
⊟ item_vector		vctr(flt, 512)	(2I1.1)
[0]		integer	

Figure 77: With vector column

```
CREATE TABLE vector.products_by_category (
item_id int,
item_color text,
item_name text,
item_category text,
item_vector vector<float, 512>,
PRIMARY KEY (item_category,item_id)
) WITH CLUSTERING ORDER BY (item_id desc);
```

We'll also create the SAI index that will enable us to search for ANN similarity. You can choose which similarity function you want to use for the ANN algorithm:

```
CREATE CUSTOM INDEX IF NOT EXISTS ann_index
  ON vector.products_by_category(item_vector)
USING 'StorageAttachedIndex'
  WITH OPTIONS = { 'similarity_function':
'COSINE' };
```

Valid values for the similarity_function is COSINE (default), DOT_PRODUCT, or EUCLIDEAN. While inserting the data, we would need to embed the images, so we can use one of the embedding models for images (clip-ViT-B-32) from Hugging Face. Hugging Face serves as a platform and community for machine learning (ML) and data science, assisting users in constructing, training, and deploying ML models. It offers the necessary infrastructure for demonstrating, operating, and implementing AI in real-world applications. Additionally, it allows users to explore a variety of models and datasets uploaded by others. Here is an example using Hugging Face:

```
model = SentenceTransformer('clip-ViT-B-32')
img_emb1 =
model.encode(Image.open('product1.jpg'))
```

Next we embed some product images by using Python:

```
model = SentenceTransformer('clip-ViT-B-32')
img_emb1 = model.encode(Image.open('image1.jpg'))
img_emb2 = model.encode(Image.open('image2.jpg'))
img_emb3 = model.encode(Image.open('image3.jpg'))
img_emb4 =
model.encode(Image.open('image4.jpeg'))
img_emb5 =
model.encode(Image.open('image5.jpeg'))
img_emb6 =
model.encode(Image.open('image6.jpeg'))
img_emb7 = model.encode(Image.open('image7.jpg'))
image_data = [  (5,'cream', 'product1.jpg',
'shirt',   img_emb1.tolist()), (6, 'cream'
,'product2.jpg','shirt',   img_emb2.tolist()),
(7, 'green','product3.jpg', 'shirt',
img_emb3.tolist()), (8,
'green','product4.jpeg','shirt',
img_emb4.tolist()),  (9, 'pink','product5.jpeg',
```

```
'blazer', img_emb5.tolist()), (10,
'pink','product6.jpeg','blazer',
img_emb6.tolist()), (11, 'pink','product7.jpg',
'blazer', img_emb7.tolist())
]
for image in image_data:
    session.execute(f"INSERT INTO
{KEYSPACE_NAME}.{TABLE_NAME}
(item_id,item_color,item_name,item_category,item_
vector) VALUES {image}")
```

Now, we can load a new image and search the database for the top similar products in the same category. By partitioning the table by item category and accessing through this partition key, we will have a better performance. Let's search the vector database:

```
def _run(self, img_path,img_category):
    KEYSPACE_NAME = 'vector'
    TABLE_NAME = 'products_by_category'
    model = SentenceTransformer('clip-ViT-B-
32')
    img_emb1 =
model.encode(Image.open(img_path))
    image_data = [(1,
img_path,img_category,img_emb1.tolist())]
    for row in session.execute(f"SELECT
id,name, item_category,item_vector WHERE
item_category={img_category} FROM
{KEYSPACE_NAME}.{TABLE_NAME} ORDER BY item_vector
ANN OF {img_emb1.tolist()} LIMIT 3"):
        result = row.name
            # display image

st.image(config['image_inputdir']+result,
use_column_width=True)
        return result
```

Logistics

The logistics industry is heavily dependent on real-time data tracking and analytics. Timely and accurate data is critical for vehicle tracking, vehicle status, and warehouse management. With its distributed architecture and high scalability, Apache Cassandra is an excellent choice for managing real-time logistics data.

```
CREATE KEYSPACE IF NOT EXISTS LogisticsGeo WITH
replication = {'class': 'SimpleStrategy',
'replication_factor': 3};
USE LogisticsGeo;
```

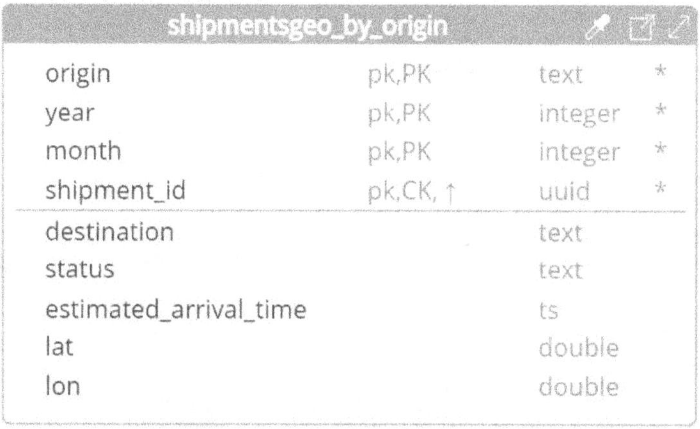

shipmentsgeo_by_origin			
origin	pk,PK	text	*
year	pk,PK	integer	*
month	pk,PK	integer	*
shipment_id	pk,CK, ↑	uuid	*
destination		text	
status		text	
estimated_arrival_time		ts	
lat		double	
lon		double	

Figure 78: Warehouse management real-time logistics data.

```
CREATE TABLE ShipmentsGeo_by_origin (
    origin TEXT,
    year INT,
    month INT,
    shipment_id UUID,
    destination TEXT,
    status TEXT,
    estimated_arrival_time TIMESTAMP,
    lat DOUBLE,
    lon DOUBLE,
    PRIMARY KEY ((origin, year,
month),shipment_id)
);
```

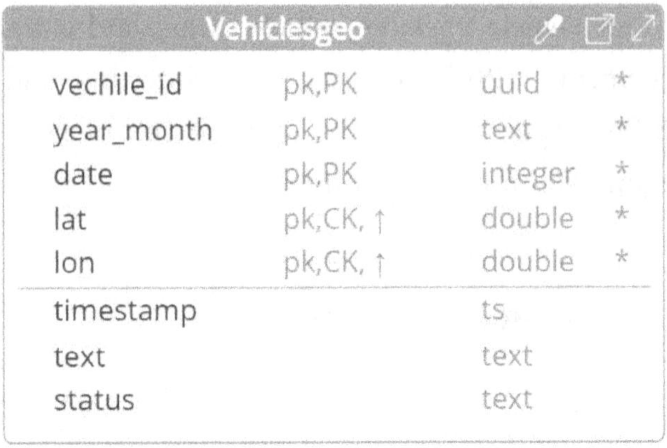

Figure 79: Vehicle status real-time logistics data.

```
CREATE TABLE VehiclesGeo (
    vehicle_id UUID,
    year_month text,
    date int,
    timestamp timestamp,
    type TEXT,
    status TEXT,
    lat DOUBLE,
    lon DOUBLE,
PRIMARY KEY
((vehicle_id,year_month,date),lat,lon)
);
INSERT INTO ShipmentsGeo_by_origin
(origin, year, month, shipment_id, destination,
status, estimated_arrival_time, lat, lon)
VALUES
('San Francisco', 2023, 11, uuid(), 'New York',
'In Transit', toTimestamp(now()), 37.7749, -
122.4194);
INSERT INTO VehiclesGeo
(vehicle_id, year_month, date, timestamp, type,
status, lat, lon)
VALUES
(uuid(), '2023-11', 20, toTimestamp(now()),
'Truck', 'Active', 34.0522, -118.2437);
```

It is possible to create a SAI index and use it
on the columns that are not in the primary key:

```
CREATE CUSTOM INDEX shipmentsgeo_lat_idx ON
ShipmentsGeo_by_origin (lat)
USING 'StorageAttachedIndex';
```

```
CREATE CUSTOM INDEX shipmentsgeo_lon_idx ON
ShipmentsGeo_by_origin (lon)
USING 'StorageAttachedIndex';
SELECT * FROM ShipmentsGeo WHERE lat > 40 AND lat
< 41 AND lon > -75 AND lon < -73 ;
SELECT * FROM VehiclesGeo WHERE status =
'Available' AND lat > 41 AND lat < 42 AND lon > -
88 AND lon < -86 ALLOW FILTERING;
```

User-item interaction

It is essential in today's digital world to understand user preferences. Online stores like eBay must track customer preferences. This creates the opportunity for more effective marketing campaigns, user analytics, and recommendation systems. In this scenario, users can "like" different items on a platform, such as an online marketplace like eBay. The data model should capture information about users, items, and their interactions (likes).

We will see a data model that manages the following tasks in Cassandra:

- Q1: Retrieve a user by user ID.
- Q2: Fetch an item by item ID.
- Q3: Get all items a particular user has liked on a specific day.
- Q4: Retrieve all users who have liked a specific item on a specific day.

Figure 80: This table captures simplified version user-specifics.

```
CREATE TABLE IF NOT EXISTS User (
   UserID UUID PRIMARY KEY,
   Name TEXT,
   Email TEXT
);
```

Figure 81: Simplified version about items.

```
CREATE TABLE IF NOT EXISTS Item (
   ItemID UUID PRIMARY KEY,
   Title TEXT,
   Desc TEXT
);
```

Q1: Retrieve a user by user ID:

```
SELECT * FROM User WHERE UserID = ?;
```

Q2: Fetch an item by item ID:

```
SELECT * FROM Item WHERE ItemID = ?;
```

User_Item_Like Table: The heart of the interaction, this table captures which user liked which item.

ID: Unique identifier for the interaction.

UserID: Refers to the user who liked an item.

ItemID: Points to the liked item.

Timestamp: Captures when the like action took place.

user_interaction_by_day			
user_id	pk,PK	uuid	*
year	pk,PK	integer	*
month	pk,PK	integer	*
day	pk,PK	integer	*
item_id	pk,CK, ↑	uuid	*
interaction_time	pk,CK, ↓	ts	*
interaction_type		text	

Figure 82: User interactions by day.

```
CREATE TABLE user_interaction_by_day
( user_id UUID,
item_id UUID,
year INT,
month INT,
day INT,
interaction_time TIMESTAMP,
interaction_type TEXT,
PRIMARY KEY ((user_id, year, month, day),
item_id, interaction_time)
) WITH CLUSTERING ORDER BY (item_id ASC,
interaction_time DESC);
```

In this example, the composite partition key consists of user_id, year, month, and day. This allows us to bucket interactions by day.

The clustering columns are item_id and interaction_time. This ensures that interactions for a specific item on a specific day are stored together and sorted by the item_id and the time of interaction.

The interaction_type might represent actions like 'clicked', 'purchased', 'liked', etc.

To query interactions for a user on a specific day, you'd use a query like:

```
SELECT * FROM user_interaction_by_day WHERE
user_id = ? AND year = ? AND month = ? AND day =
?;
```

Q3: Get all items a particular user has liked on a specific day:

```
SELECT ItemId FROM user_interaction_by_day WHERE
user_id = ? AND year = ? AND month = ? AND day =
?;
```

Q4: Retrieve all users who have liked a specific item on a specific day:

The partition key for the first table doesn't work for this query. We can create a new table partitioned with **ItemId**.

users_by_itemid			
item_id	pk,PK	uuid	*
year	pk,PK	integer	*
month	pk,PK	integer	*
day	pk,PK	integer	*
user_id	pk,CK, ↑	uuid	*
interaction_time	pk,CK, ↓	ts	*
interaction_type		text	

Figure 83: Users by item.

```
CREATE TABLE users_by_itemid
( user_id UUID,
item_id UUID,
year INT,
month INT,
day INT,
interaction_time TIMESTAMP,
interaction_type TEXT,
PRIMARY KEY ((itemId, year, month, day), user_id,
interaction_time)
) WITH CLUSTERING ORDER BY (item_id ASC,
interaction_time DESC);
SELECT UserID FROM users_by_itemid WHERE itemID =
? AND year = ? AND month = ? AND day = ?;
```

Depending on your use case, you may decide to bucket by hour, day, week, or month. To match your requirements, choose the partition key appropriately. Remember that the primary aim of time bucketing is to ensure that individual partitions don't grow too large and remain manageable.

We've prepared a data model that captures user-item interactions while ensuring fast query performance. Whether you're building a recommendation engine, a social media platform, or an online marketplace, understanding and effectively capturing user interactions is the key to success!

Three tips

1. **Design for query access patterns:** In Cassandra, creating the right data structure for your queries is critical. To do this, first, get a clear picture of how your

app will ask for data. Then, pick the best partition and clustering keys and columns to store your data so that it's evenly spread out and easy to find. Carefully choose your partition keys and clustering columns to ensure even data distribution and efficient querying. Consider denormalizing your data based on performance needs. When you design your data setup with your queries in mind, you'll make Cassandra work its best, giving you super-fast performance.

2. **Master Cassandra patterns:** Carefully calculating partition size, selecting the optimal partition key, leveraging bucketing for large partitions, choosing the right compaction strategy, and using Time to Live (TTL) judiciously can transform your database performance. Additionally, strategic denormalization can enhance query speed. However, beware of antipatterns such as lightweight transactions, materialized views, secondary indexes, and excessive tombstones. By adopting effective patterns and avoiding antipatterns, you'll be able to fully utilize the capabilities of Cassandra, guaranteeing exceptionally fast queries and scalable data management.

3. **Explore Cassandra's tools and solutions:** Check the Spark Cassandra connector for seamless data integration with Apache Spark, and leverage Stargate APIs to simplify application development. Data migration tools streamline moving data to Cassandra,

while benchmarking tools fine-tune performance.
Hackolade and Chebotko's Diagram offer valuable
insights into advanced Cassandra concepts. By
embracing these tools and solutions, you'll unlock
Cassandra's full potential and optimize your data
operations.

Three takeaways

1. In Cassandra, don't think of data modeling as just
   creating tables. It's about crafting a blueprint that
   matches how you ask for data in your app. This step is
   incredibly important. When you craft it right, your
   questions get quicker answers, your app runs
   smoother, and it can grow seamlessly. So, by focusing
   on designing your data to match your questions,
   you're essentially building a Cassandra database that
   keeps your data safe and delivers it lightning-fast and
   reliably, making your app a top-notch experience for
   users.

2. In Cassandra, patterns are your reliable companions on
   becoming a database expert. Carefully calculate your
   partition sizes, choose the best partition keys, use the
   right compaction strategy, and use bucketing
   techniques for handling large partitions. Use Time to
   Live (TTL) to manage your data's lifespan and simplify

your data structure for better performance. However, be cautious and avoid antipatterns. Actions like lightweight transactions, materialized views, secondary indexes, and excessive tombstones can lead to slow performance and persistent issues. By adopting effective strategies and steering clear of these problems, you'll elevate Cassandra to a high-performance platform that effortlessly scales and serves your application smoothly.

3. In Cassandra, consider tools and solutions as your reliable companions, equipping you with efficiency and knowledge. Establish connections with Spark Cassandra for robust data processing, easily utilize Stargate APIs for smoother app development, and smoothly transfer your data with Cassandra migration tools. Enhance performance with benchmarking tools and explore valuable insights from resources like Hackolade and Chebotko's Diagram. By fully embracing these tools and solutions, you'll tap into Cassandra's true capabilities, becoming a master of data management and gaining deep insights into this powerful database system.

Index